Learning to Teach Adults

Learning to Teach Adults is an indispensable guide for anyone who teaches, or is planning to teach adults. This comprehensive yet light-hearted book gives sensible advice on the business of teaching and training, and is relevant for any subject taught, be it archery or zoology. Writing with passion and humour, the author provides helpful tips, ideas and practical examples throughout.

Topics include:

- adult learners and learning styles;
- teaching methods and techniques;
- course and lesson planning;
- student motivation and participation;
- dealing with awkward situations.

Fully updated the new edition includes vital new sections on assessment, teaching students with learning difficulties and the impact of new technologies on teaching and learning. This engaging and accessible book is essential reading for anyone teaching adults for the first time. It is also a useful reminder of good practice for experienced teachers and trainers and a helpful refresher for anyone returning to teaching after a career break.

Nicholas Corder is a former trainer of FE tutors at Buckinghamshire LEA, and latterly Warwick and Oxford Brookes Universities.

For my wife Pauline, who teaches me something new every day. Soon, I will have mastered washing-up and ironing.

Learning to Teach Adults

An Introduction

Nicholas Corder

Routledge
Taylor & Francis Group

LONDON AND NEW YORK

First edition published 2002

Second edition published 2008
by Routledge
2 Park Square, Milton Park, Abingdon, Oxon. OX14 4RN

Simultaneously published in the USA and Canada
by Routledge
270 Madison Ave, New York, NY 10016

Routledge is an imprint of the Taylor & Francis Group, an informa business

© 2002, 2008 Nicholas Corder

The right of Nicholas Corder to be identified as the author of this work has been asserted by him in accordance with the Copyright, Design and Patents Act 1988.

Typeset in Times NR by Keyword Group Ltd
Printed and bound in Great Britain by Antony Rowe Ltd, Chippenham, Wiltshire

British Library Cataloguing in Publication Data
A catalogue record for this book is available from the British Library

Library of Congress Cataloging in Publication Data
Corder, Nicholas.
  Learning to teach adults : an introduction / Nicholas Corder. — 2nd ed.
      p. cm.
  Includes bibliographical references and index.
  1. Adult education. 2. Effective teaching. I. Title.
  LC5215.C675 2008
  374—dc22   2007021861

ISBN10: 0-415-42362-7 (hbk)
ISBN10: 0-415-42363-5 (pbk)

ISBN13: 978-0-415-42362-5 (hbk)
ISBN13: 978-0-415-42363-2 (pbk)

Contents

vi *Contents*

List of Figures

Acknowledgments

First of all, I must thank all the people I've worked with in adult education over the years – tutors, managers and students alike. I'm certain I've learnt far more from them than they have ever learnt from me. I have also learnt a great deal from all sorts of people with whom I discussed the book for both this and the previous edition. Their own experiences of learning and teaching helped to shape what I have written.

However, there are some whose contributions to the preparation of this book have been way beyond the call of duty. So, many thanks go to all those who brought me up-to-date on various bits and pieces and made encouraging noises. Katy Newell-Jones, formerly of Oxford Brookes University, persuaded me to write this book and then gave valuable insights that have made it a much better book. David Ewens of NIACE also made copious sensible comments about the manuscript at various stages. These last two have curbed my wildest excesses and put me (nearly) on the straight and narrow. I would like to thank all of them.

My wife Pauline locked me in a small dungeon whilst I wrote this book, but at least pushed cups of tea and ginger biscuits through the small flap in my cell door. She also read over the manuscript making tutting noises, but I suspect that she may just have had something stuck in her teeth.

Lastly, I'd like to thank you the reader for showing the taste and discernment needed to buy this book like this, or at least borrow it from a library or steal it from a friend's bookshelf. You are a giant amongst Lilliputians.

Preface

Those who can, do …

There's an old saying in education: 'Those who can, do. Those who can't, teach. And if you can't teach, you teach teachers.'

Writing a book about how to teach is a huge act of hypocrisy. I don't want you to think that I am the world's greatest teacher of adults. I'm not. I don't want you to think I have a huge fund of theoretical knowledge either. This book is based on over twenty-five years' experience. I've been involved in just about every aspect of adult education there is, from cleaning the classrooms as a teenager to managing a large adult education centre.

On the way I've taught all sorts of different people and some of them have even learnt things. Often, despite my interference. During that time, I've made more mistakes than I would ever care to count. I've watched people teach who can knock me into a cocked hat. I've been in lessons that were so bad the teacher should have been hung, drawn and quartered publicly. In fact, I was the teacher in some of them. I still bear the scars.

This book is the book I wish I'd had when I started teaching adults. Teaching is a practical activity and I've tried to make this a practical book. If you want a technical book full of jargon, gobbledygook and words you've never heard of, put this book down immediately. I'm really sorry, but you're looking in the wrong place.

I'm not knocking theory. There is a huge amount to be learnt from it. But the teacher faced with a class of adults for the first time is likely to be much more concerned with how to write on the board than they are with *Zabrinski's Hypothesis on Coaxial Andragogy in a Multi-disciplinary Context*.

This is a simple, straightforward book that will give you some of the basics. It's not designed to baffle you. If you want to be able to use words like 'cognitive dissonance' or 'cathexis', you'll have to buy another book. You can buy this one as well, but it won't tell you what cathexis means, because I don't know myself. I do know what cognitive dissonance means, but I don't want to show off right now. I've put it in a little glossary at the back of the book in Appendix B. I hope it's helpful.

There are many ideas in this book, but it is not a subject-specific book. It won't tell you how to teach Fork-lift Truck Driving or Accountancy or Needlework. You need to take away some of the ideas presented here and apply them to your own situation.

Don't worry about reading it in one sitting. You'll only get fed up. There are 60,000 odd words here (some of them very odd) – it's a lot to manage in one go. Pick and choose. If a bit bores you, skip it and come back to it later. I've written it in the order that I think is logical. My logic may not be the same as yours. It doesn't make either of us wrong. If you find my chapter orders daft, read it in the order you think is most logical. I won't be offended. Let's face it – I won't know!

All of us teach in different circumstances. In a short book, I can't deal with the difficulties of teaching highly specific topics such as how to deep-sea dive safely. You need to adapt to the circumstances in which you find yourself teaching.

Your right to disagree

You have every right to disagree with what I say in this book. You can groan at the bad jokes or reach for the hand-grenade. Whatever you do, please think about what I have to say.

The best teachers think about what they are doing all the time. Their styles may differ wildly but what they have in common is that they are thinking teachers who are always looking for new approaches and ideas and who listen to their students. I hope that this book helps you with that process. It won't teach you everything you need to know. I would be a fraud and a charlatan to make a claim like that.

The last chapter of the book, Chapter 10, offers some exercises that you might like to do. They're not compulsory. Some of them need a pen and paper – many of the others are simply ideas for you to think about and mull over. If you're on a teacher-training or training-the-trainer course, they're the kinds of things you might like to discuss with your fellow students over a cup of coffee at your break time.

It's not a bad idea to buy a smart note-book to keep your comments and ideas in one place. You could even keep it alongside you as you read this book. It's up to you. Above all, please enjoy the book. I hope I've made it fun to read. If when you've finished, you think, 'Well – it's nearly all common sense really', I'll be thoroughly happy. Most teaching is common sense.

Good teaching is good teaching

We live in an age of technology. You can telephone anyone almost anywhere in the world. You can email your best friend on the opposite side of the globe at the stroke of a few keys. Your car barks at you to turn left in 300 yards. We watch revolutions and wars as they happen. When I wrote the first edition, personal CD-players were the thing, now it's MP3 – you can fit your entire music collection on a device light enough to qualify for ordinary postage. Similarly, whilst computers were coming to the fore, they used to be confined to specialist IT suites. Now, they're in many standard classrooms and conference facilities. Laptop computers cost less than many televisions. By the time you read this ... who knows? Perhaps they'll have even cured the common cold.

Classrooms, lecture theatres and training rooms are also changing. We have introduced machinery and equipment that were unheard of a generation ago. You can even do courses via the internet and not meet the person who's teaching you. But, no matter how many blinking lights, computer terminals or interactive DVD players with sensurround feelorama we put in our teaching rooms (even if those 'rooms' are virtual), some things remains constant.

- Every good class is run by a good teacher.
- It's the human element that pulls it all together.
- We all know from our own experience as learners how important it is to have a good teacher.

We still remember the inspirational teachers of our childhoods. When we go on a course it is the tutor who makes or breaks the experience.

Like a lot of jobs, the people who are good at it make it look easy. We like to think of them as 'born teachers'. I'm sure they exist – I've even seen a tiny handful in action and would have swapped several body parts to be as good as they are. There are also some people who couldn't teach to save their mother's life. We should probably bar them from crossing the threshold of a classroom. The rest of us straddle all levels of expertise in between, from the adequate to the very good. Sometimes we're anything from adequate to very good in the same week or even in the space of a couple of minutes as we move from an excellent activity to a poor one.

We are the people who can be shown how to improve our teaching. We have some natural ability, but knowing a bit more will help us enormously. We are interested in our students. We want them to learn. We want them to be able to make ashtrays, speak French, pass their financial exams, comply with Health and Safety requirements – whatever.

We all make mistakes. If you learn some of the tools of the teacher's trade and have a positive attitude towards your subject, your students and their work, then your mistakes won't matter so much. I know it's a bit of a clich, but we do learn from our mistakes. Just make sure you learn from your successes as well.

Alas, poor adult education

At the time of writing, adult education is going through one of its cyclical periods of upheaval. 'Adult education is on its last legs,' goes the cry. It's always on its last legs. Read any general introduction to the subject written in the last forty years and you'll see the same prognosis. For decades the doom-mongers have been warning that 'this will spell the end for adult education', 'this' being whatever the latest government initiative happens to be. These last legs have lasted a long time.

Somehow or other, like a mutating virus, education for adults changes, adapts and becomes a slightly newer version of what it was before. It has to really;

otherwise we would still be crammed into Working Men's Institutes watching lantern slides whilst listening to a man in a tall hat murmuring on the subject of 'The horseless carriage – a noisy gimmick that is totally impracticable as a means of locomotion'.

The truth is that non-accredited provision is currently facing a tough time – of that there is no doubt. The current trend to test, measure and record performance is endemic throughout modern life in the UK and many other countries. Politicians love to be able to quote statistics on how much better, bigger or 'more efficient' something they've mauled and mangled now is, than it was when they left well alone. (Strange how they never seem to measure their own performance!) The Government wants everyone to be 'qualified', which results in certificates, records of achievement, and diplomas that have sprung up purely to meet the needs of course-providers (colleges, adult education centres, continuing education departments and universities, etc.) to act as a magnet for whatever public funds might be available.

I myself have a certificate in Small Group Work – whether this means I'm allowed to work with larger groups or not, I have never found out, but I'm a whiz with up to six people. No-one has ever wanted to see it. 'Aren't you being a bit cynical?' I hear you whimper from behind a stack of forms that need filling before lunch. Yes, of course I am. A system that is prepared to reward achievement at all sorts of different levels is far better than the educational model that prevailed in previous generations. More importantly, as jobs are no longer for life, the person who left school as early as possible is not necessarily excluded from education for ever; often they were in the past. It's just that all these bits of paper …

Still, this is the world into which you are going to venture if you are new to the teaching of adults. Yes, it might be more bureaucratic than you could imagine and you'll certainly have your fill of felled trees. But, if you don't like it, then you can always strike out on your own and form your own classes, which may of course, be the solution for all those 'non-accredited' or 'leisure' classes.

Before you get carried away with loads of paperwork or envision your new teaching empire (Village Hall, Thursdays 7.00–9.00), you might find reading this book useful. I hope so. However, it is meant only as an introduction – hopefully a practical one. If you are intending setting out on the path of becoming an adult educator, then there are other books that deal with the subjects I discuss here in more depth. I still hope it makes for useful reading, though.

A rose by any other name

Lastly, coming from an adult education background, I tend to use the word *tutor* or *teacher;* occasionally I use *trainer.* As far as I'm concerned they mean more-or-less the same thing, so they're all pretty much interchangeable. There is a host of words for what we do. All of them carry connotations – some good, some bad. Whichever word you use, someone is going to pull you up on it. *Teacher* makes you think of school teacher. *Tutor* smacks of Oxbridge colleges. *Trainer* sounds like a soccer coach. I don't like the word *lecturer* because it implies that all you're going to do is lecture. I dislike the word *instructor* even more – flat-pack furniture has instructions. My pet hate is the word *facilitator* because it is so ugly, even if the idea – that you're enabling education to take place – is a good one. *Educator* sounds pompous; *master* sounds like you know everything and *mistress* sounds like a kept woman.

Whichever word you use to describe yourself, you should always bear one thing in mind – teaching and learning are too important to be taken seriously – they should be fun.

Good luck!

Nicholas Corder

1 Adults as learners

The best days of our lives?

When we are children, our parents have the unpleasant habit of telling us that our school days are the best days of our lives. To an extent, this is true. Being forced to wear school uniform may seem pretty depressing at that time, but it's not as bad as when you're grown-up and you have to pay bills, act responsibly and start every sentence with 'In my day...'. It just seems bad at that time. For some, distance lends enchantment. Our schooldays become one long, golden period of sunshine and success, no matter how awful they were at that time.

On the other hand, many of us had some pretty miserable times at school. After all, there is only so much boredom, bullying, exam pressure, algebra and puberty you can take. However, some of us, whether we liked school or not, were able to succeed to some extent or other. We left school with some decent qualifications and were set up for a life of choices.

Even if we are reasonably successful, there are some activities that we dread. If you're confident with the spoken word, you might be quite happy to go off and learn a language, or study literature or history. If you're happiest tinkering with car engines, then stripping a central-heating boiler will probably seem fairly straightforward. But, put yourself in a slightly different set-up and your blood can run cold. Stick me in a practical class and I'm petrified. If anyone utters the words 'Today we're going to learn how to do mitre joints', I break out in a cold sweat and foam at the mouth.

Other people were not even this fortunate. They may never have found inspiration in anything. For them, learning later in life can often be a way of repairing the damage caused at school. Early disaffection sometimes translates itself into a thirst for learning later in life.

Most importantly, no matter what our educational backgrounds and experiences, all of us are capable of enjoying the buzz of learning something. We are pleased – often thrilled – when suddenly we find that we are able to do things we couldn't do before. Ordering from a menu in Spanish, reversing a caravan, knowing the capital of Norway – all these improvements in our skills and capabilities give us a sense of achievement. Some of us may need more help or more time to get there, and sometimes we may fall short; but learning gives people pleasure.

Take a look at your adult class, or if you're not teaching at the moment, think about a class you've attended recently. Whoever those adults are; whatever their experience, background and achievements; whatever their abilities, capabilities and skills; they have two things in common. They have come to the class and they are adults.

What is an adult?

I've been using the word 'adult' very freely. Perhaps it's time to take stock and see if we know what we mean by the word. After all, this book is about teaching adults, not children (although some of the content is still relevant to the teaching of children).

We all know that there are differences between adults and children. We know that adults think, act and speak differently now from when they were children (except for a number of reality television show contestants). It would seem reasonable, then, to suppose that the way in which we would want to be treated as learners would be different as well. So, if we're going to think about what an adult is, where should we start?

Age

An easy way of defining adulthood might be by age. On the surface that seems straightforward enough. So what age shall we use? The age for sexual consent? The age when you can start to drive or vote, or the age when you are old enough to join the army? Perhaps we'd like to ignore all of these and to use the old voting age – twenty-one. Maybe we wouldn't consider anyone under the age of twenty-five mature enough to be considered an adult.

It would be very difficult to come up with a definition of adult by age. You as the reader might say simply 'Well, you're old enough to vote at eighteen, so that's what we'll call an adult'. Someone else's experience of eighteen-year-olds might be that they find them extremely childish. There is, for instance, a difference between a group of undergraduates (even those who've had a gap year) and a group of experienced health workers on an in-house training course.

So perhaps what looks like a straightforward, nice, easy answer isn't as simple after all.

Maturity

In that case, maybe we should look at the idea of maturity. We then run into the problem of defining that word as well. After all, we know some adults who are very childish and some teenagers who have acted as if they were middle-aged since birth. It is also possible for someone to be mature in many ways, but imma-ture in others. If you take the obvious signs of maturity, like marrying and having children, then that could mean that the young mum of twenty-three is theoreti-cally more mature than the maiden aunt of seventy. Difficult, isn't it?

Life-cycle

We could decide if someone is an adult by using the major events in people's life-cycles. Everyone goes through a series of stages in their life. Obviously, the cycle starts in infancy, when we are totally dependent on adults to feed and clothe us and to keep us warm. Then we move through various phases until, unfortunately, we go off to meet our maker. There are dozens of theories about what happens in-between (as well as loads of after-life theories!). In fact, so much has been written about it, that it has become a field of study in its own right. All of the specialists recognise the fact that as we go through adulthood we change, which is quite obvious really. However, the way in which this is expressed differs quite greatly.

In the financial industry, the life-cycle is often lumped into four straightforward chunks. Here, they ignore childhood altogether, probably on the basis that children (in the main) are more likely to buy comics, sweets and gizmos, than they are to set up their own hedge-fund company. The first stage in the financial cycle is when people are setting out on careers and suddenly have large areas of expenditure, such as cars and housing. The second is when they're shelling out for children and general family expenditure. The third is when they are likely to have both their highest income and their least expenditure. Lastly, comes retirement, when they are drawing on financial planning schemes, pensions, savings and the like.

That's straightforward enough if you want to judge whether to sell someone a long-term savings scheme or an instant-access account, but seems perhaps a little limited as a complete descriptor of our lives.

One of the most influential thinkers on life-cycle is an American academic called Dan Levinson. He wrote a book called *The Seasons of a Man's Life* in 1978. He divides adult life into eight phases – four transitional periods

- early adult
- age thirty
- midlife
- age fifty.

Plus four stable periods

- novice
- settling down
- renewal
- legacy.

Levinson's ideas are quite complex, but in essence the phases of life he describes are:

Early adult transition (age 17–22)

In this phase you are leaving adolescence behind and taking your first few steps in the adult world.

The novice phase (age 22–28)

At this stage, you begin to develop your dreams about the way you would like your life to develop. Often, we find some kind of mentor in our personal or professional lives – or both. We also start to make choices about our careers.

Age 30 transition (age 28–32)

Towards the end of our twenties, we begin to realise that life is for real. This can be a stressful time as we either make new choices or get used to the choices we've already made.

The settling down phase (age 32–40)

Now, we are establishing a place in society and trying to make it in our chosen careers or jobs. At this point, we often strive for wealth or fame or recognition or social status.

The mid-life transition (age 40–45)

This is another period where we take stock of our lives. Forty seems to be the age at which we can look backwards over our lives and look forwards to what is to come. We start asking ourselves serious questions about success and failure. Many refer to this kind of age as the mid-life crisis. You know the sort of thing – you get mistaken for your mother or the face in the shaving mirror belongs to your father, so you have to buy a sports car to compensate.

The mid-life phase of renewal (age 45–52)

This is the point at which we start to listen to our 'inner voices' as it were. It's when we think of all the things we wanted to be or do and then do the ones that we still fancy, if possible. We accept our responsibilities and try to balance the different demands that home and society demand.

Age 50 transition and the legacy phase (age 52+)

Around our early fifties, we begin to think about what it is we are going to leave behind us. After which, we then move on to making sure that we leave some kind of legacy. Often the legacy phase is one of great creativity. You will find that the traditional adult education class is full of older students, partly because they have more time, but also because they seem to want to develop themselves. Often, the most energetic, creative and generous people in your class will come from this group.

Of course, we don't all fit neatly into these categories. Some of us marry later in life; some of us never have children. There are people who fulfil their early dreams; there are also millions of people who live lives of quiet desperation, suffering in jobs they hate. Some people never seem to have been young; others never seem to grow old at all.

There are also other criticisms that have been aimed at Levinson's model. The most frequently aired viewpoint is that it charts the life progression of white, middle-class, western males. Certainly, many women, who undergo the same 'development' as men, might do so at different ages, because of career breaks to bring up a family (although Levinson has since written *The Seasons of a Woman's Life*). There are cultures where it is not unusual for several generations to live in the same house, and whilst there may be some delineation of roles within that, the concept of a 'bread-winner' is irrelevant as resources are pooled and shared. I'm sure you can think of plenty of exceptions to Levinson's theory and those of his successors as much has been written about life-cycle theory in the past thirty years; it's also worth investigating the work of Merriam and Clark if this is an area that particularly appeals to you. They use life events as a way of bench-marking work-related and love-related events across one's life-span.

Even if we don't fit neatly into Levinson's (or anyone else's) phases, there is no doubt that notions such as 'being successful' change with time. We are also a mixture not only of our own personalities and our cultural histories, but influenced by the different stages at which we find ourselves in relation to family, work and others. Our concerns, priorities, likes, dislikes, tastes and opinions vary over time. Succinctly, let's just say that there are few (if any) of us who are the same people at forty, or sixty, as we are at twenty. And I'm not just talking waistline.

Forget definitions?

Perhaps the problem lies in actually trying to find an exact dividing line between childhood and adulthood, and then trying to sub-divide adulthood into component stages. It may well be that we don't need a precise definition of 'adult' after all, but we do need some idea of the typical elements of adulthood.

Think of your own life. The likelihood is that if you are reading this book you are an adult. You know you are an adult because you are over eighteen, you probably drive, you might be married, have children, have to pay VAT on your clothes, and you pay the gas bill. But, you may still have your teddy bear; you still buy popcorn at the cinema, and can't face getting rid of your train set. Then being an adult is probably a question of being more of one thing than you are of another.

So, adults often have most of the following characteristics:

- They are above the age of compulsory education.
- They have some experience of the world of work.
- They have family responsibilities.
- They have financial responsibilities.
- They have domestic responsibilities.
- They are reasonably independent.
- They are able to make their own judgements about the world around them.

- They have some experience of life.
- Their tastes are more sophisticated than they were when they were younger.

Most importantly though:

- This is not their first learning experience.

The adult as learner

When adults come to your course, they carry with them the accumulated experience of every other situation in which they have learnt something. Call it 'baggage' if you like, but their experience will, as we have seen, be a mixture of negative and positive. Your job is to make their experience of your course or class as good as you possibly can, no matter what the authorities do to prevent you from teaching well!

Regardless of where you are teaching, you will find that the students in the group have a wide range of backgrounds, ages, attitudes and experience. If you are going to be teaching a Beginners' German evening class, this will be obvious at the first meeting of the class, because you can immediately see differences in age, dress and so forth. On the other hand, if you are going to teach a group of experienced salespeople, differentiation might be harder, or more subtle. You might automatically think of those people only in terms of their experience as salespeople. Sometimes you've got to look beyond the apparent – in other words the role they play – and at the people they are.

So, who are they? As well as having gone through some elements of the formal process of education (school, college, university), the adults on your course will also certainly have learnt things in an informal setting. There are the kinds of things that one learns in the home – boiling an egg, bleeding a radiator or putting up shelves. They have often taught themselves how to do something, perhaps by reading how to do it in a book, or by adapting something they have learnt elsewhere.

In all likelihood you will be teaching in a formal setting (a classroom or meeting room), even if you do not teach in a formal way. Your students will have preconceived ideas about what to expect from the course, how they prefer to learn and the teaching methods they suppose you will use. They will also have some knowledge of the subject matter, even if they are supposedly complete beginners.

Let's examine what adults bring to their learning, for if school children are not simply empty glasses to be filled from their teachers' jug of wisdom, then the adult glass is often fuller than you would imagine. Or, to stretch metaphors even further, they are not blank canvases for you to paint on.

Knowledge

First, no matter how obscure the subject, adults almost invariably have some previous knowledge of it. Sometimes, we even know something without knowing we know it. In Moliére's play *The Would-be Gentleman*, the social-climbing Jourdain is having specialist tuition from a Master of Philosophy and discovers what the word 'prose' means. 'Good Lord!,' he exclaims, 'I've been talking prose these last forty years and never even knew it!' Similarly, I can look out of my study window and see the road, our car, flowers, bushes, shrubs and passers-by without for one moment understanding how this happens. What is the process by which light enters the eye and gives the brain these images? What biomechanics allow a passer-by to pass by? Why do those flowers bloom and die with the seasons? How does the engine of my car work? Does it need a service? Yes, staring out of the window is highly thought-provoking and a marvellous work-avoidance technique.

We also gather little snippets of information as we go about our daily lives. Let's take that Beginners' German class again as an example. First of all, it is highly likely that someone will have studied German before. It's quite common to find people who studied a couple of years of a language at school, or who recently did a year's evening class, but still consider themselves absolute beginners. These quasi-beginners already know some basic words and phrases – numbers, days of week, the names of some items of food and drink. As they themselves tell you, they have forgotten an awful lot. That does not make them *absolute* beginners. Your class also probably contains some people who have been to a German-speaking country and have picked up a smattering of everyday German words or perhaps the occasional sentence hard-learned from a phrase book. There may be ex-service people, who have served in Germany and have only a smidgen of language, because their day-to-day life was conducted on English-speaking bases, but a vast knowledge of the customs and geography of the country. They know phrases like 'Excuse me, we have just had a helicopter accident and my semi-automatic machine-gun is beyond repair', but don't know how to ask where the loo is.

Even the people who have never been abroad will almost certainly know the odd word or phrase – *Vorsprung durch Technik, Blitzkrieg, Auf Wiedersehen, Achtung.* Then there are the international words, which although sometimes spelled differently, they will recognise – *Café, Theater, Telefon, Bus, Computer* and so forth.

Your students may not know a lot about a subject but at least they know something. Each student's knowledge is going to be different from that of his or her neighbour.

Experience

If all adults already have some knowledge, they also have some degree of experience. Let us stick with our Beginners' German class for a moment longer and take a chap called Peter as our example. Now, Peter knows as little German as it is possible to know. However, he did study French to O-Level (the precursor of GCSE for any of you youngsters reading this) at school in the days before the world turned lax and sour. Despite his lack of knowledge, Peter has experience of learning a language and that experience will either help or hinder his learning in your class. If his previous experience was positive, then he is likely to be able to transfer those skills to learning the new language. If his experience of learning French was poor, then he might find it makes it harder to learn. He may also have learnt the language in a way that gave him plenty of formal grammar skills, but left him feeling inadequate when it came to speaking. Anyone who has ever heard recordings of Winston Churchill broadcasting to the French will understand what I mean.

Essentially, our previous experience is crucial for our development, and experience is hard to avoid. In fact, let's face it, the average adult would have to have lain in a darkened room for several years not to have picked up a huge amount of experience (and even then, they'd have experienced darkness and lying down).

In a television documentary a few years ago, a very young doctor (actually he looked like a teenager, but then we're all getting older) was on his way to visit a woman who had recently given birth. He confessed that he was single, had no personal knowledge of babies and that he found it very worrying when asked by mothers for his advice on such matters. Essentially he was admitting he knew less than the mother. Now, nobody is going to argue that there is not some advice he could give, after all he probably knows better than the mother the symptoms of, for example, whooping cough. However, she is also an expert; she has the first-hand experience. She's the one who pushes when the midwife says 'push'.

It seemed to me that the doctor was looking for a partnership with the mother and this is a crucial idea in all forms of education, but at its most obvious with adults. You must make your students your partners in the learning process. In some ways, this is getting harder to do as more and more courses aimed at adults carry qualifications. There is thus less freedom to explore tangential topics, ideas, activities and interests. That doesn't make it impossible. My young journalism students are expected to write newspaper and magazine-style articles as assessed work towards their final degree mark. If no-one in the group is remotely interested in writing a sports report, then my running a session on sports-reporting will be less useful than running one on, for instance, travel-writing, when 90% of the group fancy writing about exciting destinations.

As a young tutor of French to a group of Francophiles, I was always being asked about areas of France I had never visited and other aspects of the country of which I had no knowledge whatsoever. To begin with, I felt rather 'put on the spot' and did a great deal of bluffing, but after a while, I realised that the class's knowledge of the country complemented my knowledge of the language. They taught me a great deal about the regions of France. They didn't mind that I didn't know; they were pleased to be able to show off a bit of knowledge.

When you teach a group of adults, you must bear in mind that they are all experts. By that, I don't mean that they are all necessarily leading lights in their profession or highly skilled craftspeople, but they all have life experience. They can do things you can't; they know things you don't; they are experts in life.

Imagine you are going to teach that group of experienced salespeople we had earlier. They're starting work as mortgage consultants and you need to teach them the legal aspects of mortgages, purchasing a house, and so on. You are an expert on the legal side of house-buying, but some of the students/sales team will have bought their own houses and/or have mortgages of their own. There might even be someone who has done their own conveyancing. There is, therefore, a great deal of expertise within the group. What a shame not to make the fullest possible use of it.

Celebrate the differences of knowledge, skills, aptitudes and abilities within your group. Involve your students.

Commitment

When an adult embarks on a course, he or she is making an impressive commitment. In the majority of cases, adults have paid for the course they are taking themselves, and even if they haven't they probably need to follow the course for reasons of personal or professional gain. Seldom is an adult coerced into going on a course, so your students are likely to be volunteers.

This is very different from school. It may not be good practice, but the teacher of a reluctant school pupil can always fall back on coercion as a bottom line. As a tutor of adults, you cannot do that. You simply can't treat adults like infants. A friend of mine, Suzanne, recently started a full-time nursing course. She has three young children and used to have a responsible job. In the second week of the course, she arrived a couple of minutes late (her train was delayed) and her tutor started banging on about punctuality and commitment. No one's doubting that punctuality is essential (especially if you're going to be a nurse), but the tutor had not looked beyond the obvious. How much commitment does it show if you give up a job, commute an hour each way every day and juggle the heavy domestic responsibilities which come with having three children under the age of seven? This kind of comment would be enough to put many a stout-hearted student right off. It could ruin a less confident student's career. And, yes, punctuality is important, but you (the tutor) must be punctual too. Indeed, when my friend David was working as a tutor-trainer in an FE College, he always started his sessions bang on time, thereby leading by example. We're all capable of 'do as I say'; it's better to be able to 'do as I do'.

Forget any ideas about being able to force your students to do anything. The nursing tutor didn't help Suzanne to be more punctual; she merely made her resentful, upset and has created a potential long-term problem on a three-year course. It is far better to inspire and enthuse your students. You need to build up their confidence, not knock them down.

A successful tutor is one who can harness the enthusiasm of students and allow them to grow and develop by the skilful use of a wide variety of techniques. But don't forget that we all interpret our experiences differently. One person sees a situation as a challenge; another as an insurmountable problem. Often, our most anxious students prove to be under-estimating their skills and abilities. Most of us need encouragement, warmth, humour, commitment, enthusiasm and a sense of purpose to engage with our learning.

On the other hand, if you want a class full of carping, grousing, whingeing, self-absorbed moaners, who fail to make progress, then the best way to achieve this is by ensuring that you are badly-organised, under-prepared, dismissive, dour, humourless and that your classes largely consist of your aimless twittering. A positive attitude from you will transfer itself to your students. In the main a happy class is happy because you're doing the right thing. When I was the manager of a large adult education programme, we always had a rule of thumb. A class that moaned a lot was taught by a tutor who moaned a lot. The good tutors passed on concerns so they could be dealt with, nipped problems in the bud and ran happy, cheerful classes that people really wanted to attend.

Yes, there will be exceptions to this rule. Life wouldn't be thrilling without them. Sometimes, if people are attending one of your courses against their will, better judgement or whatever, it can occasionally make life tough for you as a tutor. There are also people who are simply difficult to deal with. We'll look at the types of students who can cause problems in Chapter 3. But they are rare in any form of adult education, although that in itself is difficult as it gives you less chance to develop the skills of dealing with them!

Confidence

Often, adults lack confidence. Their own experience of formal education might be poor. They are frightened of failing. They don't want to hold themselves up to possible ridicule.

As adults, we learn things in an almost haphazard way, even if we do fit what we learn into some kind of framework. In other words, we are used to learning in our own way and in our own good time. When we enter an unfamiliar situation, we feel fear, apprehension and anxiety. We either withdraw into ourselves or find ourselves trying to show off what knowledge we have to compensate for these feelings of inadequacy. The students in your class are no different from us, they too might initially try to over-compensate. Quite simply they are anxious and nervous, because they are unused to formal learning and possibly new to the subject (at least in a formal setting). They may even have studied the subject at school and failed at it or might have had a very unsuccessful educational career to date. They may have used up so much of their courage in actually turning up for the course, that they are unable to participate until you have enabled them to feel more relaxed. They need to feel at ease, valued as members of the group, and that you are interested in them as people.

Don't forget that we are also all products of our gender, race and class. We are influenced by past learning, success (or lack of it), confidence levels, our surroundings, our support mechanisms at home for our course of study. We're also suddenly thrown in with a group of people whom we may not know (or for that matter like) and who all, no matter what course you do, seem so much better and cleverer than we are.

All these factors influence the way we learn; we're all the same – we're different!

A quick summary

So, that's a brief guide to adults as learners. We are all products of our environment, our genes and our experiences; so are your students. Their ages, tastes, perceptions, politics, attitudes, knowledge, experience, aptitude, ability and intelligence (and the list could go on) are all different. They may well be at very different stages in their lives. They will all have different needs and make different demands on you.

It is with this wonderful mixture of people in mind that you have to start planning your course. Do whatever you can to draw on their skills, knowledge and experience and take a positive approach to your teaching and your subject.

But before we start planning what we're going to teach, it's worth having a look at what we mean by learning; how people learn both as individuals and in groups; and at a variety of teaching methods.

2   What is learning?

In the Middle Ages, philosophers and theologians would argue over the number of angels who could dance on the head of a pin. Trying to define learning seems a bit like doing that. As with all these things, academics debate long and hard, adding new theories and hypotheses until their definitions become extremely complicated as they end up looking for a definition that will cover all eventualities. However, it is important to try to understand what we mean by the term.

Inevitably, whenever you start getting into the theory, you end up using the jargon of the trade. There is a jargon-buster at the back of the book. Jargon is a double-edged sword. On the one hand, it's useful as it gives practitioners a common language; on the other hand it's all too often obscure, elitist (in the worst sense of that word) and smug.

I hope we're not counting angels here, because the concept of learning is central to the idea of teaching adults. We want our students to learn something. If they don't, our classes are a waste of time and we might as well be at home watching reality television. One common fallacy is that theory is somehow separate to practice. It isn't. Theory tends to be a way of being able to make comments about what happens in the real world. So, for instance, a bit of minor economic theory would be that if a product is in short supply, then its price will rise; if it is plentiful, the price will fall – the law of supply and demand.

Types of learning

For many of us, the word *learning* has associations with *memorising*. You *learn* your times tables, the alphabet, the dates of the Tudor Kings and Queens. But learning is not just a matter of acquiring new knowledge. We can also learn how to take someone's pulse or how to deal with an awkward customer last thing on a Friday afternoon without resorting to physical violence.

Learning also carries with it the idea of developing something – a skill, knowledge, the power of argument. We can improve our Hungarian goulash, grow more colourful roses, put up stronger shelves and make longer words at Scrabble. In other words, we can also learn how to do something *better* or *more efficiently*.

When we teach our students, we're going to expect them, by the end of the course, to be able to do something that they couldn't do before they came to our class, or to do it better, or sometimes (such as in a keep-fit class), maintain a level of skill.

Be careful about using the word 'learning' too much in your classes. You'll be surprised at how frightening the idea can be for some students. If you wonder why this is, just think about how we talk about learning in everyday speech. If we say, for example, 'I learnt Spanish at school', it carries with it the idea that we can remember some. We tend to say 'I did Spanish at school' and that way, if someone asks us an awkward, tricky question in Spanish, such as 'What's your name?' or 'Where do you live?', we don't feel embarrassed if we can't reply.

Teacher trainers often divide learning into three main types of skill – psychomotor, cognitive and affective – although often the skills overlap.

Psychomotor skills are concerned with physical abilities. Learning how to swing a golf club is a psychomotor skill, as is improving your netball or learning how to ride a bicycle.

Cognitive skills are concerned with developing and increasing knowledge. If we find out how to calculate Standard Deviation or the dates of the Tudor Kings and Queens or what colour of electrical wire signifies neutral, then we have increased our cognitive skills. However, unless we actually understand the purpose of Standard Deviation, the relevance of Tudor chronology to the development of that era and the effect of wiring a plug properly, then we're dealing purely in information. Information is generally worthless unless you can actually do something with it.

Affective skills are concerned with a change in attitude. Often these are the most difficult skills to learn as we have such an emotional attachment to our existing ideas. Learning to tolerate the foibles of our neighbours is an affective skill. Allowing others to talk in a group, when we desperately want to throw in our opinions all the time, is also an affective skill.

If you want, you can refer to these three types of learning as skills, knowledge and attitudes.

Obviously, there are times when you are going to have to learn using all three domains. Learning to drive a car involves psychomotor skills – you have to steer, change gear and work the pedals. It also requires cognitive skills – you have to understand what various road signs mean. It may also involve affective skills – someone who thinks that driving fast is safe, needs to understand the potential consequences and dangers of speeding.

Memory

Memory plays an important part in the learning process. There are essentially three stages to the memorisation process. You have to input information, store it and then retrieve it – rather like a computer.

There are then two main sorts of memory – short-term memory, where we hold facts and ideas for as long as we need to apply them and long-term memory, where we store information for use at a later stage. So, for instance, knowing where the bonnet catch is on a car hired for the weekend is not as useful in your long-term memory as knowing how to get at your own car's engine.

If we are to 'learn', then we have to transfer information, knowledge and skills into our long-term memory. This means that we have to practise what we have learnt – often in a variety of situations, in order for it to be of long-term use for us. In the main, it's almost impossible to separate out these stages as they are so closely linked. If we do break it down into these steps, we probably do so subconsciously.

In our house we have a place where we're supposed to keep our keys. I know this, because the whereabouts of the key-box is seared into my long-term memory. Right now, I cannot find my car keys. Not having stashed them in the box, I can't for the life of me remember where I put them. This is either my short-term memory letting me down or a failure on my part to retrieve information. I will then go through various memory-jogging techniques, such as retracing steps, thinking where I last had them, lifting the enormous piles of paper from my desk – you know the sort of thing.

We all develop different techniques for memorising information. As we enter adult life, we find fewer and fewer opportunities for actually sitting down and memorising. There are people who like to teach themselves poems. Actors have to work at learning their lines for a play. Most of us don't have to go about learning in this way. We absorb information, without realising we are doing it. We know the name of the Chancellor of the Exchequer, because we hear the name repeated so often on the news. We can recite the names of the 1966 World Cup winning side, although we've never sat down and consciously memorised them. Ply a middle-aged man with drink and he can recite the whole of the Monty Python dead parrot sketch.

But here lies the key to memorising information – and indeed to an extent applies to all three learning domains. Repetition is crucial. Now, that doesn't mean that you should get your students doing some rote learning, like you did at primary school. It does mean that you have to think about ways of teaching the same thing several times, without it appearing that you are repeating yourself. This may sound rather boring, but it actually means that you can come up with interesting ways to cover the same ground. It also means that you can appeal to the different kinds of learning styles.

Learning styles

None of us learns in the same way. We all remember the childhood friend who just had to take the radio apart to see how it worked, or the bookish one who knew everything, or the child who was genuinely motivated by the thought of a gold star.

Over the years, we all develop different approaches to learning. Psychologists and sociologists can argue forever about whether this is due to our nature or the way we are brought up. It's a fascinating debate, for which there is not enough room here. What does matter is that you are likely to find yourself with a class of people who all want to learn in slightly different ways.

There are several academics who have researched the concept of learning styles thoroughly. One of them, Peter Honey, identified four basic styles. The names he gives for each of these categories are activist, theorist, reflector and pragmatist. Whilst the jargon might sound a bit off-putting, it's a very useful reminder of how different we all are. As you read, try to see what categories you think are most apt for you. You'll probably see yourself as a little bit of each, but with a definite preference for one or two styles.

Activist learning style

An activist, as the word suggests, enjoys active ways of learning. They love new experiences or having fresh problems to solve. They thrive on the excitement of the moment and enjoy being part of a team. On the other hand, they're not happy when they have to work on their own, have to follow precise instructions or sit and listen to lectures. They need to be able to join in. An activist is not necessarily an 'outdoor pursuits' type, s/he simply likes getting stuck in and getting oil up to the elbows.

Theorist learning style

There's nothing theorists like better than to have their minds stretched and challenged. Analytical, happier with complex ideas, they are at home testing out assumptions. They're largely unswayed by emotions. They would rather be dealing with ideas than their feelings. It's no use asking them for a snap decision, they need to be allowed the time to examine their subject in depth. Stick a theorist in with a bunch of bustling, busy activists and s/he will truly feel ill-at-ease. That's a shame as the activists could have rushed off to build a suspension bridge that won't work, by the time the theorist has calculated that you need a cantilever bridge instead, and done the designs.

Reflector learning style

The reflector likes to have plenty of time to observe what is taking place before embarking on a project. Happy undertaking dogged research with few time constraints, they feel at ease when they can cogitate and chew over what they are doing. They don't like it when you give them a deadline, or expect them to do something spontaneously. Ask a reflector to do a role-play, for instance, and they will probably want to write themselves a script first.

Pragmatist learning style

Pragmatists like to be able 'to see the point of something'. They're the ones learning French for their holidays, rather than for the fun of it. They like to know that there is some practical, useful output at the end of a course. They thrive on plenty of practice and often need strong guidance as to how to complete a task. Don't expect a pragmatist to cope well with theory. Anything that doesn't look like real life can put them off completely.

To sum up, here's a little tale I was once told. An activist, a theorist, a reflector and a pragmatist all decide to learn golf. The activist gets out on the course and keeps on swinging at the ball until he gets the feel for it. The pragmatist books a set of lessons from the pro. The theorist reads up on trajectory, wind resistance and anatomy before taking to the course. The reflector ends up caddying for the other three, so he can watch them close up before having a go himself.

Of course, there are other psychologists who have investigated learning styles and come up with their own theories. You may come across such names as Fry, Gagné, Belbin, Bloom and many others. They all have worthwhile ideas about learning and you should read up on their ideas if you are to take your professional development any further.

No matter which set of theories you like (and there are plenty to choose from), the main point is that we are largely some kind of mixture of different learning styles. It's highly unlikely that we're entirely theoretical in our learning, or totally pragmatic. All of us are likely to learn using a variety of styles. It is very rare indeed to find someone who does not possess at least a trace of the qualities of each of these learning styles. However, we probably favour certain styles over others. This book is written from a pragmatic point of view. Teaching is a largely pragmatic activity and, as a pragmatist myself, I hope that I can understand that people need to learn in different ways and apply that knowledge by using a range of activities. But that's just me. If you are more of a reflector-theorist, you will probably find that you will want to read up on some of the theories that I have mentioned in passing. If you are more of an activist, you probably just want to get into the classroom and get on with it.

None of these learning styles is wrong or better. As students, if we can extend our learning styles, we have the chance of learning in a wider variety of situations. We often use different styles depending on what we are doing. Teaching ourselves the guitar, we are probably being activists. Reading up on the education of adults and we are being theorists. We are reflectors when we research and write essays. We are pragmatists when we memorise the times of the commuter trains that will take us to work. (Or perhaps we're actually being pragmatists if we don't memorise the train times, on the basis that they never keep to them!)

As teachers, tutors or trainers, we have a responsibility to ensure that we appeal to the whole range of learning. It's a pound to a penny that your class will contain students whose learning styles will differ wildly. I would also suggest that we have a responsibility to expose our students to other ways of learning than those they are used to. Broadening the ways in which we learn can only do us good.

The learning cycle

Of course, all this makes is sound as though we learn things in a vacuum. We don't. If I learn that my unmarked jug will take half-a-litre of milk, by calling on past experience, I can also reckon that it will take half-a-litre of orange juice or water or gin. If I know that there is a speed camera at the end of my road, I refer to that knowledge no matter what car I'm driving.

One of the most interesting theories of learning is that of David Kolb. He describes what he calls the 'learning cycle'. Kolb's idea is that we continually develop as learners, but that in order for our learning to be effective, we have to ensure that we go through a cycle. We experience something, we reflect on it, we form abstracts concepts about what we've experienced and then we act on it. Kolb's major point is that we can join in this cycle at any point. We can start with a concrete experience or a simple abstract concept, but as we work round this cycle, testing out our ideas and knowledge in different situations, then we learn. So, for instance, if someone shoves a flute in your hands, with the instruction 'Play!', we're actually acting before we've observed what to do. In other words, the cycle is a process of refinement that involves thinking, observing and doing.

Interestingly, all the various theories of learning and the learning cycle are currently being reappraised. Amongst those examining them sceptically (remember that scepticism is not the same as cynicism), is the excellent Phil Race (www.phil-race.com). Race's books and website are excellent for anyone starting out, filled with practical tips and ideas for teaching, which you can use or adapt to suit yourself or your students.

Motivation

In the same way that adults have different experiences, knowledge and styles of learning, so their motivation for attending a course can vary a great deal. Again, there are many theories of motivation – Maslow and Herzberg are two of the best known figures in this area of study.

Amongst adult educators, it is generally accepted that adult learners fall into two broad motivational categories. The first type of motivation is normally called 'instrumental'. Someone whose motives are instrumental is likely to see your course as a means to an end. They probably have specific goals in mind: 'I want to be able to do my own accounts' or 'I want to learn how to bake a carrot cake'. Again, these are quite pragmatic desires. They want some kind of concrete outcome from their course.

Many of us want qualifications – another instrumental motive. We need them for our work, to help us get or change jobs or win promotion. Occasionally, we just want to prove to ourselves that we are capable of studying to a given standard. We all need our self-esteem boosting from time-to-time. I once had a phone call from a lady who had never obtained a qualification in her life. Now, well into her fifties, she'd passed an elementary Spanish exam. She was so thrilled; I couldn't get her off the phone for half-an-hour.

For some people, qualifications are the be-all and end-all of education. This is a pity. Sure, it's difficult to dabble at an art class if you're out of work and need English and Maths GCSE and a computing qualification to stand the faintest chance of getting a job. However, there's nothing wrong with learning for its own sake. This is something that I fear will disappear as the middle-classes overload their children with extra-curricular activities (thereby potentially putting them off for life) and adults can only take courses that give them a piece of paper (some of which are, bluntly, entirely worthless).

This paper-chase can inhibit those learners who have 'intrinsic' motives. They are learning the subject for learning's own sake. 'I've always been fascinated by history and wanted to find out more about the Victorian sewerage system of Greater London'.

Some people regard learning as part of being a 'whole person'. Many of us grab the adult education brochure the minute it appears in the library and scour it avidly to see what we might dabble in this year. It's not uncommon to come across someone who has used their local Adult Education Centre, Further Education College or whatever, to learn a huge range of skills – holiday Spanish, basic car maintenance, crafts or psychology.

The subject of your course may simply interest them. They want to know about the geology of the Lake District or how to mend a sewing machine. They are happy to extend their knowledge. They may also be learning or polishing a skill for the sheer pleasure of increasing their expertise.

Some students are plain curious. Some want new experiences all the time. For some it is the realisation of a dream. 'I always wanted to write, but I never had the time.'

The social gathering

I think that in local adult education, there is also a third group. Your local Adult Education Centre, often run in a school or as part of a FE College's provision, tends to be a fairly gentle place. It's not going to be top of your list if you want to drink a gallon of lager, eat a fistful of kebabs and get in to a punch-up. It's a good environment in which to meet people semi-socially and there are plenty of people who attend their local adult education centre for social reasons.

People who have recently moved to a new area often look to adult education as one way of kick-starting their new lives. You will also find people who suddenly realise that their lives are centred on work and feel the need 'just to do something else for a change'.

Some come because it's convenient. The class they really want to do is in another town, they haven't got transport and they can walk to yours. There are other students who try a different course every year, for whatever reason. They may be looking for something that takes their interest, or are happy dabblers. Not everyone feels the need to be an expert. Some of us are content to feed our general knowledge and skills at a surface level.

Sometimes husbands and wives come to the same class in order to get some time together. There are young mums who take classes to keep their minds active, and dads who escape family commitments one night a week. There are couples who take a break from each other. It's easy to think ill of these people, to dismiss them as 'dabblers', especially if you are particularly precious about your own subject. We worry that they will be the ones whose attention and motivation may be hardest to capture. Surprisingly, they often turn out to be the best students. As they are there for social reasons, it is often they who suggest going for a drink after class or arrange the end-of-term meal. They are often keen to make the most of their opportunities. They give the group an extra, informal dimension.

Mixed motives

Of course, these descriptions are generalisations. We can have all three types of motivation – instrumental, social and intrinsic – at the same time. 'I want to study A-Level Psychology to get into university. I've always been interested by the way people think and act. Meeting other people who are fascinated by it as well is tremendously helpful. I tried studying on my own, but find I like the encouragement of being in a group.'

Similarly, motives can alter over time. 'I fancied doing a spot of flower arranging just as a bit of a change. I found I loved it and now I'm going to take some formal qualifications because I want to become a florist.' Our floating socialites get the bug for local history and produce a definitive guide to their village's Civil War past. Our *Computers for Work* students find new friends who share their hobbies in internet chat rooms.

It is important that we understand our own students' motives. We need to understand why they are attending our classes in order to be able to plan properly for them and to teach them well. Let's look at a case study to see what brings them in.

The bricklayers—a case study

Imagine for the moment that you are teaching an evening course on bricklaying. If you ask your students why they've come, you might well get answers like these:

- I want to build an extension to my house.
- I'm new to the area and want to meet new people.
- I always do something on a Monday.
- I wanted to be on the general DIY course, but it was full.
- My husband and I always do the same course.
- If I can put up something that will stop my neighbour sticking his nose into my garden every five minutes, I'll be happy.
- I'm a keen gardener. I want to landscape my garden and put in some low-level walls.
- I've just retired and found I've never really had a hobby, so I thought I'd try this.'
- I always do a different course every year.
- I'm busy all the other nights.
- I spend all day sitting at a desk. I never do anything physical. I need a break.

Looking through this list, you might think that only a few of the students are there to learn bricklaying. As a Companion of the Golden Trowel (First Class), you might be dismayed that they don't seem particularly interested in your pet subject. But people's motives for attending a class are often much more complex than they seem on the surface. Besides, they have all *chosen* to learn bricklaying and parted with money in order to do so. You have to balance all the learning *needs* of the group.

You must consider what individuals within the group have in the way of previous experience. In the group above, you might be in the situation where nobody has laid a single brick or knows a single word of the terminology used in bricklaying. This does not mean that your students come without previous experience. The DIY enthusiast may be used to working with his/ her hands and learning a huge range of different practical skills compared with the person who is normally desk-bound. Similarly, the student who intends building an extension is either being very naive about the amount of work it will take to undertake such a task or has a huge level of confidence. If it is the latter, compare this with the couple who always have to do things together.

It's compulsory

On the other hand, you may find yourself faced with a group who have been forced to come to your class. This could be for any of a variety of reasons. For example, regulatory bodies often demand new forms of certification. Some organisations' training programmes are compulsory. This often means that people have to attend courses to get new qualifications or to prove that they can do something that they've been doing perfectly well for years without anyone interfering. They might even resent you.

So, it's important to bear in mind that students will be in your class for a wide variety of reasons. It's vital therefore that you should make sure you find out why they came as early in your course as possible. You can either do this formally, within the session, or on a less formal basis.

Learning isn't straightforward

Learning anything new is a complex process. Moreover adult students are unlikely to be on your course as their primary activity. They have jobs, families, houses to look after. They may have sick relatives or shift patterns that mean they can't attend as regularly as they would like. Even the keenest part-time adult student has a million other things to do before they come to your class.

Learning is hard, but there are additional reasons why some students will find it harder than others. Not everyone can boast that they have had good experiences of learning in the past. Anyone who had a miserable time of it at school is going to find it hard to re-enter a formal educational situation. Simply being in a classroom is stressful – especially if it is a borrowed classroom used in the evenings in the very school in which they feel they did so badly.

Often adults lack confidence in their own ability. They have never been able to compare themselves against others, so they have no idea how good (or very occasionally how poor) they are. Many of us come from a background in which learning and education are seen as important. This isn't just so that we can get better jobs. We visit museums, or watch plays. We want to know the names of plants, the stars in the sky and the opening times of the local library. There are millions of people for whom such a culture does not exist. You might want to stereotype them as the ones who are always glued to their television sets, mistaking celebrity gossip for real news and singing along to the advertising jingles. This does not make them stupid. What it might mean is that there is no support for them if they go to learn something at a class.

There are also people from 'intellectual' backgrounds who regard manual skills as demeaning, just as much as there are people with practical skills who regard book learning as 'airy-fairy' and a waste of time. There are also people for whom memory, or even basic intellectual skills are a real problem. We are not all brain surgeons and rocket scientists. You have to cater for as many people as possible.

Special educational needs

Some people have additional needs that make it very difficult for them to learn in conventional situations. Whilst this book is not about adults with specific learning difficulties, it is very important to be aware of the subject. We can only touch the tip of the iceberg in this book, so if you're going to work in this area, you really do need to seek out specialist advice, reading matter, knowledge and help.

Most organisations ask students when they enrol if they have any additional needs, or would like to disclose anything. The institution should then pass on any relevant details. However, this presupposes that the student has officially enrolled (rather than turned up on spec), has mentioned anything (they may not want to commit it to paper) and that the original form still exists within the Byzantine world of educational administration.

Sensory impairment

If someone is hard of hearing or has impaired vision, then they might find some aspects of your lessons difficult to follow. If a student tells you about this kind of disability straight away, it isn't necessarily a problem. They will soon let you know how you can help. Often this will involve simple, common-sense adjustments, such as seating the student close to you, or simply making sure the lights are switched on in your teaching room. You may have to speak up a little or make your handwriting on the board larger. 'My handwriting's awful—can everyone read that all right?' is probably just a touch more sympathetic than 'Can everyone SEE that all right? What about you, Betty?'

If you've got access to a clever photocopier, you can have handouts blown up larger, or print out directly from a computer using a larger font. If you're demonstrating something allow a person of restricted sight to handle what you are using, if it is possible and not too dangerous. It's also worthwhile flagging up any hazards around the room that might be especially difficult. You can always give yourself a taste of what it's like by putting a patch over one eye for a day. Just see how often you miss the coffee cup handle.

When students are not forthcoming about these problems, it can be difficult. Again, if you encourage students to let you know (privately if necessary) if there are any difficulties, you will usually find they are quite forthcoming. You can easily adjust your room layout to accommodate them.

Other students are almost always extremely helpful and kind. You'll always find volunteers to carry bags, fetch a cup of coffee or help out in whatever way they can. They can even be a little too zealous at times. Most problems become invisible after a while. I had a lady in one class with nerve problems in her neck. Every now and again she took herself off with an upright chair to lean against the wall. No one paid the least attention to it.

Basic skills—literacy and numeracy

Many people in this country (and throughout the developed world – we're not the exception) have missed out on a decent basic education. Every now and again, some survey or other will hit the headlines, declaring that an enormous percentage of the population is *functionally illiterate*. What this means is that they are supposed not to possess the basic skills of reading and writing that are needed to operate in the modern world. Everyone then bemoans how appalling the state of education is, chunters on and a few days later it's forgotten.

Of course it's nonsense. Most people develop enough literacy skills to manage, even if they cannot spell perfectly or hand-write in awkward capitals. Many learn how to disguise their difficulties. Often, the wife or husband will have dealt with the paperwork. They are far less likely than someone with, for example hearing problems, to come forward and tell you their difficulties. They may well have developed an enormous range of practical skills, skills that many more bookish people would be thrilled to possess. Often, they disguise their lack of literacy by using the famous 'I've forgotten my specs' routine. The more ingrained the habit of avoiding the written word, the harder it may be for them to admit they have a problem.

Most importantly for you, is that you need to be aware that many people have not progressed their literacy skills as much as they might (for whatever reason) and may need particular help. Don't be fooled by appearances. I know of one tutor of basic skills who visits a small mansion in order to give its self-made multi-millionaire owner lessons on very basic writing skills. The man can add up (that's how he made his fortune), but even as the owner of a large company, he has real difficulty with very basic written English.

These difficulties are much more likely to emerge if students are taking a course that involves a good deal of reading, or using the written word. They may struggle on a word-processing course, with a modern language or local history. It's perhaps less obvious if they are learning how to rock climb or to cook Indian food.

However, there is a lot of information that we tend to give in written form. The cookery class will have recipe sheets. The rock climbing class will probably have handouts on safety or the care of equipment. These students may struggle to understand them.

Similarly, large numbers of people are unable to manipulate basic figures. Adding, subtraction, multiplication and division are alien to them. Those people who can multiply multi-digit sums in their heads often cannot conceive of anyone who doesn't seem to be able to grasp the most fundamental arithmetic concepts. When faced with numbers, especially serried ranks of them, they too can easily feel tremendously intimidated. We need to take into account these people's difficulties as we go about our business of teaching. We must be sympathetic to their needs and adapt our materials to their particular situations.

Dyslexia

The word dyslexia is of Greek derivation and means 'difficulty with words'. People with dyslexia often show a huge gap between their intelligence and their work on paper, have difficulty organising themselves, poor short-term memory, severe difficulties with spelling and their handwriting is frequently poor.

The latest thinking on the subject would indicate that there is some kind of mismatching between the two hemispheres of the brain, so that the right side (which deals with areas such as creativity) is more developed than the language-oriented left side.

The problem with Dyslexia is that in many ways it's an exaggerated form of what most of us frequently feel like. Dyslexics typically have poor concentration, are slow readers, have difficulty organising, sequencing, processing and remembering information. They are likely to be poor at time management and, perhaps the most obvious sign for a tutor is that their spelling will look like a bad Scrabble hand. Note-taking can become a big problem, as are subjects where there is a lot of reading.

The British Dyslexia Association reckons that around 4 per cent of the population are severely dyslexic and that a further 6 per cent have mild-to-moderate problems. In theory, then, a group of ten adults is likely to contain a student with some level of dyslexia. This may not be the case, but you should be aware that people in your group may be dyslexic. Some will be forthcoming about their difficulties; others may try to hide them. Some may not be aware that they have a problem, especially if their schooling dates from the days when they were simply labelled 'stupid'. Anecdotally, many dyslexics seem relieved to have a name to put on their condition. It's a little bit like being diagnosed with a disease; until the doctor's done that, she can't prescribe a cure.

There are certain straightforward strategies you can adopt to help dyslexic students. First, you should be as encouraging and supportive as you can without singling out the individual too obviously. If possible, rely on the advice and guidance of the student, if they are prepared to give it. They know their own problems best. Bear in mind that a dyslexic student needs structure to their work. They are usually happiest and learn best with active tasks that are not just paper-based. Often, a dyslexic student will find that a hand-held tape-recorder, a portable computer and some kind of organising system such as file dividers or a personal organiser are a positive start. Some like handouts and worksheets to be printed out on coloured paper. If you can, provide both written and spoken versions of what you are doing. You may find that the most useful support you can give is actually in helping the student to organise their work, such as ensuring that they know hand-in dates for assignments, rather than worrying about the odd car-crash sentence.

Dyslexics also like to know what they're going to do before they do it. It's not a bad habit to tell your students what you intend doing in a session – the problem is that this often changes. If you do need to change activities, make sure everyone is aware. 'That took a bit longer than I'd expected, so I think it's best if we come back into a big group now and look at X instead of Y.'

As for reading, this is not always the problem you might assume. Handouts are useful to dyslexic students as they reinforce work done in class. Reading out loud is, on the other hand, probably one of the things that they fear most. If you do read out in your class, ask for volunteers, anyway. In fact, doesn't most of this sound like basic good practice anyway?

Where to go for support

If you find someone with dyslexia in your class, or you suspect that someone might be dyslexic but does not realise it, then you will need to do further research on the subject. There are some useful contacts in Appendix A and further reading in the Bibliography. If you are working in a larger institution, you may find some-one with specialist knowledge who can give you more direct help. Similarly, the Basic Skills Agency (see Appendix A) publishes a whole range of guides and useful materials, so if you need more detailed information, it is worth investigat-ing them. If you are working in a Local Education Authority or in a Further Education College, you may even be able to get a classroom assistant to support you.

The emphasis is very much on inclusion. We want everyone to stand a chance of participating in the educational system – and quite rightly too.

Age

Our age also makes a difference to our ability to learn. Our physical abilities decline with age. Given that a professional footballer typically retires in his early thirties, you can be fairly sure that most adult students are beyond their physical peak! Bits of us (especially hair and teeth) drop out. Where once we might have been able to identify the sex of a bluebottle at thirty paces, now we're hard put to find our spectacles. Our reactions slow down, our hearing becomes more muffled and our hand-eye co-ordination can deteriorate. If that wasn't enough to put up with, we also have to submit to the ignominy of being worse at some mental tasks. We can't memorise facts like we used to be able to.

The good news is that all is not lost in our advancing years. We may not be as sharp as we once were, but we develop better strategies for many tasks. Memory isn't necessarily that important. If you don't know where Ulan Bator is, it doesn't matter, so long as you know where you've put the atlas.

The increased general knowledge that we pick up as we go through life, and our ability to organise ourselves better than we could as children, certainly helps us to manage our learning. We understand more. We sift information for the most important bits. We have developed systems for coping with our weaknesses and inadequacies. Whenever you see some child prodigy on the television, they are nearly always mathematicians. A young child does not have the breadth of knowledge and experience that older people have. It may be unusual for a child of ten to get A-Level Maths; it would almost be impossible for them to get the equivalent qualification in a subject that demands life experience, such as History, Social Sciences or Literature.

So, although age can be a barrier to learning, there are also advantages to being an older learner.

Successful learning—what you can do as a tutor

So, there they are. There is your class full of students, with all their different expectations, educational levels, intelligence, motivation and difficulties. All you have to do now is teach them.

It's a tough job. As a good tutor, you want your students to learn as much as they can. You want them to be happy in your class and to feel as though they are making progress. You want them to take a positive attitude to the subject and to look on you as a good tutor.

There are many things that you can do to ensure that your students get the best learning experience they can. Students need motivation. We all learn best when we have clear reasons for learning something. It doesn't matter whether these are for pleasure or for work; we learn best when we know why we are learning something.

As we have seen, not all students arrive at adult education with the kind of motivation that you might want them to have. So, you have to motivate them. Students like 'good' teachers. So how are we going to define a 'good' teacher?

A recurring theme of this book is the importance in getting the atmosphere right in your classroom. Your attitude is the largest possible determinant of the group's attitude. You may be teaching in an old ramshackle hut with mould patches on the wall, but if you bring a lightness of spirit to your work, your students will hardly notice their surroundings.

You also need to have a good knowledge of your subject. Realistically, you can't be expected to know everything. If you don't know something, don't fudge the issue. Sometimes you will find people in your class with greater knowledge and experience in some areas than you. This is especially true if you are younger than most of your students. Draw on their expertise. Don't be threatened by it.

Students like teachers to seem well-organised. If you don't know where the lavatory is, always forget your register, are forever opening your briefcase to find you haven't brought the handouts and are constantly dropping the overhead projector on your feet, you're going to have to work extra hard to make up for it.

Students also like teachers to be well-planned. If you are one of these teachers, you will often get compliments. Take the attitude that if you show your students that you are working hard for them, then they will work hard for you.

If we like praise as tutors, then it is logical that we also like it as students. As a tutor, we should be handing out constant praise for achievements. You can even joke about it and hand out little gold stars if you like. It catches on. In a creative writing class I used to teach, one week we all read out parts from Jim's playscript. The next week, he brought us all home-made certificates testifying that we have achieved 'Grade A in acting'. Yes, it's silly, but it's a laugh and most people enjoy it and it feels like praise, no matter how tongue-in-cheek.

Students need reminding that they have already done lots of things in their lives and learnt to do all sorts of complicated things – how to drive, how to cook, how to raise a family. Vitally, they also want you to empathise with them in their attempts to learn. This is often easier said than done. Once you have learned and practised something so often that you are perfectly capable of doing it in your sleep, you may have forgotten just how hard it was in the first place.

You need to be flexible. An approach that works well with one group or a student, may not work as well with another. You need to be able to abandon your best laid plans in order to rescue a floundering lesson. You also need a sense of humour. You don't have to be a stand-up comedian, but it does help if you enjoy a laugh. If you can laugh at yourself it's even better. When your carefully constructed scientific experiment collapses in front of your bewildered students, it's no good acting like a temperamental prima donna.

Being good at presenting your subject also helps. Of course, knowing how to set your students going on individual and small group tasks is important, but if you don't do the stand-up-and-teach bit well, then it can undermine you as a teacher. If you're not confident doing this, practise at home. You can fake confidence until the real stuff comes along.

Bringing variety to your lessons is also important. In Chapter 4 we look at a whole range of teaching methods, and in Chapter 5 we examine what learning and teaching resources are available to you. Always be prepared to try something new. Your students will appreciate the fact that you try to vary the activities in the class.

Adult students also like to feel as though they are getting support from the rest of the group. As ever, this is the elusive idea of 'atmosphere' that it is your job as a tutor to create. Managing your class well also includes getting the balance right between whole group work and individual attention.

So, teaching adults is dead easy. All you have to be is an empathetic, sympathetic, highly organised, well-planned, praising, praiseworthy, encouraging, knowledgeable and a comedic manager with decent presentation skills. In fact, if you check out Appendix F, there are even new national standards for how we're supposed to be! Oh, and of course, you could argue that you can't teach anyone anything, they have to learn it for themselves. All you can do is create the right environment for that person to learn.

It's a piece of cake.

3   Learning in groups

We've seen in the previous chapter how adult students have vastly different levels of knowledge, ability, learning styles and motivation. Teaching each type of learner on an individual basis is hard enough, so what happens when we put these people into groups?

If you are new to teaching and observe a lesson, you might find yourself concentrating on what the tutor does. Often it is far more useful to observe what is taking place within the group itself. What kind of interaction is taking place between tutor and students and amongst the students themselves?

Perhaps the first question to ask yourself is the vague one of – does the class have a good *atmosphere*? Do the students chat to one another as they arrive? Do they help each other with chairs or equipment? Does the class seem to have a social dimension to it? Do the students say things like 'There's the book I promised to lend you'?

You can also tell a great deal from the coffee break if there is one. This is the chance that most groups have to do a little socialising. Does the group feel like a social unit? How does the tutor use the break? Good tutors tend to use the break for a mixture of social chit chat, a little bit of administrative work, helping students on an individual basis and speaking to those students who perhaps did not say a great deal in class. If all of this kind of activity is taking place – if you get a sense of warmth, purposefulness, humour, helpfulness and empathy, then these are all positive signs that the tutor is encouraging the class to mix. This means that in the class itself, they are more likely to speak up, help one another out on projects and feel relaxed about the business of learning.

In the classroom itself, how many people speak during the session? Some students are bound to have more to say than others. Some of us are simply louder than others. But that's not quite the point I'm trying to make. Does everybody get the chance to say what they want? Does the tutor (or do other students) try to get everyone involved in the activities as much as possible? Do the students allow one another the opportunity to speak or do they rush in to interrupt?

Occasionally discussions can get quite heated. This is not necessarily a bad thing, but when things do get hot, do the students still respect one another's points of view?

The benefits of learning in groups

Undoubtedly, there must be benefits to learning in groups, otherwise you wouldn't find huge numbers of adults throwing themselves back into education and training each year. Nor would you find companies and public bodies funding group teaching, training and learning on the scale that they do, even if some of the courses that are funded may be of little value in themselves.

Unless you've got the sharpest focus, unwavering dedication and vast reserves of self-discipline, learning something on your own can be very dispiriting indeed. Houses the length and breadth of the country are full of unused rowing-machines and exercise bikes, dusty guitars with missing strings, old audio-cassette tapes boasting that by lunch-time you will be able to pass for a native in Andalusia and self-assembly kits that remain un-assembled. (Mind you, if they really were self-assembly, wouldn't they put themselves together of their own accord?) Self-help books designed to make us thinner, more muscular, less debt-ridden, more attractive to the opposite sex, and with a vocabulary that Dr. Johnson or Noah Webster would have died to possess stand on our shelves. A yellowing envelope marks the point at which we gave up – usually page 17, for which there must be some scientific explanation.

What this shows is that we like to learn in groups. There do seem to be advantages to it and, whether we can articulate these or not, there are several reasons why we herd together to learn. Foremost, we tend to be social animals. We like being with other people. Sharing the experience of learning seems to help us. Perhaps we simply like some company. Maybe it's because being part of a group allows us both gentle competition and co-operation. We can often learn a great deal from others who are struggling to achieve the same things. It can also help to set our own standards and it saves us the embarrassment of being singled out. We can, from time to time, hide. The group helps us to feel secure – safety in numbers.

As a tutor, do not underestimate the social aspect of learning in groups. A class you help to be non-cliquey, fun and who accept new ideas and newer students can be one of life's great pleasures. A good group, where students are supportive of one another, can help learners improve their self-image. The students will themselves become important learning resources and their encouragement will help others who are perhaps struggling. A good group can be a powerful learning resource in its own right. It gives its members mutual support, purpose and belonging to groups like this genuinely helps the social fabric. Even if the word 'community' is over-used by lazy politicians fishing for vaguely positive words, a good class becomes a little community of purpose.

Creating a good group

You thus have to do your best to get your group to gel, to respect one another's opinions, to work well and to learn together. Your group will, however, be made up of individuals. Their competing demands will have a big impact on you as a tutor.

You have to be seen to be fair, but you have to allow for all the differences within the group.

How are you to achieve this? How are you going to balance individual's needs with group needs within the overall structure of the course? How are you going to find out the needs, demands and expectations of your students?

Your group management style

As a tutor, it is your job to manage the group. Those of you who have worked for several different managers will know that management styles vary enormously. At one end of the spectrum is the tyrannical despot, who demands the impossible, expects you to guess what they want before they want it and wanted it yesterday anyway. At the other end is the weak, feeble, incompetent buffoon who would spend all day deciding whether you should order ginger nuts or digestive biscuits for the tea break.

Of course, these are extreme caricatures – most of us fall somewhere between these two. You do need to realise, however, that your management style is going to have an important bearing on the way in which your group works. And you are in charge. You're paid to be the tutor.

Just how 'in charge' do you want to be? If you want to make sure that you are the king-pin of the group, you will need to adopt a very directive style. All initiatives will come through you and your students will largely be in the situation where they are reacting to you rather than to each other. Alternatively, you might want the group to be entirely democratic, in which case you would need to play a far less dominant role, perhaps seeing yourself as some kind of neutral chair.

Student participation

A well-run class means that all your students will have the opportunity to join in. It's important that you take an approach that is encouraging, sympathetic and allows the students to learn as much as they can. This may seem obvious. I've rarely seen a tutor who doesn't try to be like this, but I have occasionally seen newer, more nervous tutors, who because they themselves don't feel relaxed, don't manage to put their students at ease.

If you've read *Animal Farm* or *Lord of the Flies*, you will know what can go horribly wrong with groups. You'd be very unlucky to end up facing a group of students, their faces painted scarlet, wielding sharpened sticks, but if you do your job badly, you may end up either with no students at all, or with a delegation of them in your manager's office. Nobody wants this.

Group dynamics

Groups take time in which to develop. They go through a variety of processes. If you've ever seen any of those television programmes where a handful of people are locked away together on a remote island, you will know that people tend to take on different roles within the group. There has been a great deal written about the roles that people adopt when they are in groups. It makes for fascinating reading and, if you are part of a particular group at work or in education or as part of a hobby, you will soon start examining who plays what role.

In a teaching group, the process is not quite the same, because you are the tutor and even if you are not directive, the students will ultimately look to you as a referee or arbiter. Occasionally, you will find some students who are more difficult to teach than others. It may seem odd, but discipline can be a concern in an adult class. I discussed this recently when I was teaching adults in a residential setting. The group I was taking was lovely – very supportive of one another and gave one another plenty of opportunity to join in. During a break, one asked me if I ever had 'problem' students as she couldn't see that if people had paid good money, they would be a problem. It seemed that her idea of 'problem' was the kind of yobbish behaviour and failure to do work that can happen at school (of which I was perfectly capable myself in my day). If you're teaching children and the worst comes to the worst, you can probably send a disruptive child out of the room or to the Deputy Head or exclude him/her from school in extreme circumstances. You can't do the same with adults (although they can be barred, in theory). Students on compulsory courses can occasionally be resentful that they are even there, but it is very rare indeed to find a voluntary adult student who is a truly disruptive influence. So, my answer to her was that it was possible to have 'difficult' students, but that whilst some students could place a strain on the group, genuinely problematic adult students were few and far between.

We're all difficult students in our own ways; we all have weaknesses, foibles and idiosyncrasies. Some of these are harder to deal with than others. When you are dealing with students whose attitudes seem to be problematic, just bear in mind that they are often nervous and lacking in confidence. It's very easy to overcompensate and that is what they are likely to be doing.

However, here are some of the occasional hiccoughs that you will encounter and you will soon find that you have students who fit into the following categories.

The leader

There's often someone who seems to want to be the leader. Sometimes there's more than one person. Often, you will find that if you are using a democratic approach, there is someone who feels that they have to take up the reins of the group because you're 'not doing your job'. You'll occasionally find that your leader is actually simply used to being in charge – someone who has been a high-ranking manager for many years, or run his/her own business – and simply falls into that role, without for a second realising that he/she is treading on toes.

In actual fact you are the leader, because you are paid to be. There may well be students in the group who think they should be the person in charge but you are the boss, even if you're not a bossy boss.

Mainly, they are looking for something to do. Perhaps they want far more out of your class than learning to make stained-glass, strip a bicycle or understand the growth cycle of deciduous trees. Talking amongst fellow tutors, we've found that if you give this sort of person a job to do, they will be truly happy and any potential problem nipped in the bud. Perhaps you could make them the unofficial social secretary of the group so they can organise the end-of-term meal, or make them your meeter-and-greeter of anyone new to the group, or tea monitor.

The clown

There's often someone who likes to tell jokes or throw in bit of humour. These students can be a tremendous help for group development, if they're doing it in the right way. After all, humour is a useful tool in the classroom. I always think that one of the best aspects of being in a group is the possibility to enjoy yourself whilst you're working and humour is an essential part of that. These students are not normally particularly difficult to deal with, unless you are teaching a group of young adults and it is the student's way of rebelling. They usually calm down after a while.

When a class comedian is not actually funny, your group will soon groan at the appalling puns. You can also limit the jokes by making a joke of it with lines like 'So, what's the joke of the week this week, Frank?' and, bless his soul, Frank will trot out the joke of the week.

More difficult to deal with is the joker who tells rude, sexist or racist jokes. Often, by not giving any reaction, the student will come to realise that such matters are out-of-order. Again, often other students will come to your rescue. If a student insists on this kind of behaviour, it's best just to have a quiet word. If anything untoward happens as a result of the 'quiet word', then pass the matter onto a manager. As a tutor, you are not paid enough to deal with this kind of thing, although these sorts incidents should not be ignored.

The inarticulate student

We all know how hard it can be to put our thoughts into words sometimes. We're forever thinking of exactly the right thing to say several days after we've had the conversation. Some students find it difficult for large parts of the time. Often, a student will have an idea, but can't express it. If another student in the group is particularly clever with words, the less articulate student can be intimidated. This is particularly hard during group discussions. A hesitant student has just as much right to join in as the eloquent ones, but may not feel able to do so. As a tutor, you have to ensure that such students are allowed their say.

If a student expresses something that doesn't seem to make immediate sense, you need carefully to pick through what they've said and then repeat their ideas back to them, without demeaning them in any way. Try not to change their ideas or embellish them – just make them clearer for everyone. As well as helping the individual student, it is also likely to help the group. Occasionally, the clever, articulate students do not have the patience for their less fluent colleagues: this method sets a good example for them.

Ramblin' Rose and Silent Sid

Never once adhering to the subject in hand, ambling off down the by-ways and cul-de-sac of whatever it is that takes their fancy; Rose uses the most far-fetched examples to baffle you and your students into complete incomprehension.

Don't feel too hard about Rose. We know that meeting new people is an important element of adult education. This may be the only chance she gets to speak to anyone all week. There's rarely any malice in her. Wait for Rose to draw breath. When she does, you have to dive in, thank her for her contribution, re-state what the group is discussing and move on. 'Can we have some other views on this?' Occasionally, your classroom Rose will able to breathe with her ears, making finding a suitable interruption point difficult. In this case, you have to have a bit of faith in yourself and simply barge in with a 'thanks, Rose, we've got a lot to get through this session, so we need to be moving on, I'm afraid'. Chances are that if Rose hasn't got the awareness that she's taking up too much time, she won't be aware of what you might consider rudeness in your dealing with her.

Silent Sid, on the other hand, is more difficult to deal with. We have to know why he is so quiet. He might be bored, in which case you need to work to catch his interest. You may have accidentally ignored him and he is feeling put out. Again, you need to try to involve him, perhaps with a direct question. Sid, like Rose, might be shy. Whilst Rose covers for this by talking too much, Sid goes back into his shell. If that is the case, he needs some gentle coaxing. Instead of doing an activity that involves the whole group, get them to work in smaller groups, pairs or individually. This generally solves the problem, if indeed it is one – some people are naturally less talkative.

The opinion seeker

You will often be asked your opinion as a tutor, because people expect you to have one. If discussing a delicate matter, try to keep your opinion as balanced as possible or clearly state that what you are giving is your personal opinion.

Normally, asking for an opinion is a genuine inquiry. Students will usually believe that your opinion is worth hearing, whether they agree with you or not. They may even want a little advice. Unfortunately, sometimes, there can be a little shark lurking a fin's distance from the surface. Some students deliberately seek out the tutor's approval by making sure that their opinions coincide with yours or are pushing you to declare that you belong to one side or another of a debate. If you think that is the case, then it is simply best to avoid giving an opinion and say that your point of view isn't important – it's the students' opinions that count.

For some discussion-based subjects, you may have to act as Devil's Advocate, prodding students into thinking more broadly about a subject by taking up a deliberately opposing view. State clearly that that's what you're doing.

The highly experienced or knowledgeable student

Students can learn a great deal from each other, as well as from you. If you are lucky enough to have an experienced and knowledgeable student in your group, with a positive attitude to the other students, you have an excellent resource. They can, for instance, be enormously helpful in practical classes, where working alongside newer students; they can be ready with a handy hint.

The problem occurs when others in the group (and sometimes the tutor) are intimidated by them. You occasionally find someone who has come to your class to show off. My mate Ian, a languages graduate, was once in an Italian class. The tutor was a native speaker who didn't spend too much time on grammar, preferring to concentrate on oral work. She wrote an example on the board. A snooty voice from the back asked:

'Can you explain to me what the gerund is doing in that sentence?'
'I'm sorry, the what?'
'The gerund. You know, the GERUND.'

The young tutor looked perplexed. She obviously didn't know what a gerund was. (Let's be honest, do you?) Ian maintains that it was one of the greatest pleasures of his life when he turned round and said, 'I think you'll find it's a GERUNDIVE'.

It's quite useful if you've got a student who can do this kind of thing for you, but it is your responsibility to handle the situation. If you have a student who is always showing off their greater knowledge or experience in a way that seems to oppress the other students, then they might be better off in a higher level class.

If not, you have to cope with them in yours. Try to show them that you are pleased to be able to use their experience, but make sure you also draw on the ideas and knowledge of others in the group.

In fact, you will normally find that your students have a far greater tendency to underestimate their abilities, than to believe they are the fount of all knowledge and wisdom. Most students will need stroking and encouragement, rather than sitting on. To mangle an old cliché, they want bouquets, not brick-bats.

The combatant

It may just be in their nature to be aggressive or heckle, but you occasionally come across students with a belligerent attitude. Again, the likelihood is that your aggressive student is as nervous as the rest and that aggression is the way in which they are compensating. On rare occasions, you will find this kind of behaviour on compulsory courses, where your student (or delegate, or attendee) simply wishes they were elsewhere.

You're paid to grin and bear it. As in all these instances, it's very easy to lose one's temper, but you have to give him the benefit of the doubt. He may be the sweetest person on the planet, but his wife has just left him, the bank's foreclosed on his mortgage and he's under threat of redundancy. He's angry and you're on the receiving end. You also need to keep the group under control. It's not going to help if they react too strongly to him either.

Instead of succumbing to the great temptation of laying into our GI Joe with a baseball bat, it's best to look for something positive in what he has to say. If you're able to pick out one or two points that you or the group can agree with, it will normally go some way to placating him. Often, your bristling student will settle down after a week or two.

The rescuer

You ask your group a question and there's a deadly silence. Is the question too hard? Should I reword it? Is it so simple, they can't believe I've asked it?

The rescuer sees you're struggling. They are the Seventh Cavalry and you are the floundering wagon train. Every time, they ride to your rescue, which means that the other students are missing out on a chance to respond.

They've got the best of intentions and they're a godsend when you're teaching a new group, but you have to try to involve the others as well. If they jump in a little too often, then crack a joke with them and say that it's about time the others did some of the work.

Side conversations

In the main, side conversations need encouraging in adult education. They are often a sign that the students are interacting well with one another, with the materials you are using and with the task you have set them. Even in whole group work, you will find that most side conversations are connected with the subject. Often it's just a case of one student helping another out.

From time-to-time, these conversations may be distracting to the other students. Occasionally, they may be personal. Only rarely are they nasty. If you find that a side conversation is getting in the way, it is often a good technique to throw out a few questions, aiming one at one of the students caught up in the conversation, without making it too obvious.

If you find that you've got a lot of side conversations happening at the same time, then there are several possible causes. Your students may be bored. They may be a little confused by what you've said. They may find the last point you've made needs more discussion. Ask if the students have understood your last point and if there any questions. If you are open to students and encourage them to ask for clarifications if they're unsure of anything, you'll find this kind of side conversation rarely happens. Generally, if you find side conversations are beginning to impinge on the session you are trying to teach, then it is time for a change in learning activity.

The clique

Occasionally, you may find that a class has a tendency to divide itself into little sub-groups. If you're teaching a weekly group, this could happen during the coffee break. This is natural enough. We tend to gravitate towards the people with whom we think we have something in common.

Those who are switched on to politics, music, film and theatre might soon find themselves in one group. Smokers, forced outside to find what shelter they can, will often band together purely because they smoke. I suspect that this is bound to happen to some greater or lesser extent. It probably doesn't matter, provided the sub-groups are not mutually antagonistic or one becomes a bit of an in-crowd. You can always mix students across friendship groups when doing work in-class or break down the class into smaller units, using your own system for devising pairs, threes and so forth.

If you do get your general attitude/atmosphere/ethos right, you will not often suffer from the clique. You are much more likely to encounter factions in established groups that you take over than you are in newer groups.

Extreme types

Occasionally, you will come across people who are impossible to deal with on any rational level. You will find the rare student who will write to you to tell you all your shortcomings; the student who is extraordinarily rude or personally offensive; or a student who manages to start putting all the other students off coming. Anyone who has taught adults for a number of years will know that there is a tiny handful for whom nothing you do will work.

I strongly suspect that if you are a decent tutor, who listens to your students, is open, helpful, encouraging and, to be blunt, good at what you do, then the fault actually might just lie with the student. This may seem like heresy in some quarters, but we can't, in the end, be everything to the students in our classes, much as we might try. It's hard to ignore how hurtful these people can be, especially if you are a conscientious tutor who tries to do the very best for your students. Don't punish yourself endlessly about the matter. It may be small consolation to tell you that we're all affected by this kind of thing from time-to-time. Sometimes, it really isn't anything you've done!

Welcoming a newcomer

Not all students join courses right at the start. This can be awkward for everyone. Sometimes a group may feel already established; at other times an extra student may unbalance the group in some way. The main difficulty is likely to be for the new student. Put yourself in their shoes. How would you feel? Most of us will be a little apprehensive, a little self-conscious, or even downright nervous. Our minds will be full of little niggling worries. We are the interloper, the stranger. We have a whirl of queries. Will everyone be more advanced than me? Have I missed too much? Can I catch up? Will they all know each other? Will they accept me? We don't want to feel different, isolated, an outsider.

Your job as a tutor is to integrate the newcomer into the group as quickly as possible. It's not a bad idea to start any new term by stating that new and old are equally as welcome. If term is already underway and a new student arrives, take a few minutes out from what you are doing to get the group to introduce themselves to your newcomer and vice versa. The new student will probably forget all the names straight away, but at least they'll feel as though everyone's making an effort, and some of your existing students will at least remember his or her name.

If you can, pair the student up with a tame student of a kindly nature, who you can rely on to be encouraging. If at all possible, try to see the new student alone for a few minutes at some point early in the first session and certainly in the coffee break, if you have one. Try to catch them up (very gently) on what they've missed and give them any handouts that cover what you've done already. Use existing students as a resource. If any jargon words or technical terms come up, ask your 'old' students to explain them to the new one. This will help integrate the student and also act as a useful revision exercise for the rest.

Make sure the student is aware of the plan that you have for your course and what s/he can expect to achieve at the end of it. The warmth of your approach to the student will be normally be picked up by the group and they will soon be welcomed into the fold. Again, at the risk of repeating this *ad nauseam*, groups will take their lead from you.

Effective communication in the classroom

Communicating to a group is very different from dealing with people on an individual basis. Good communication is essential to running a good class. For a start, you need to be able to ensure that your voice carries to all the students in the room. This is not too difficult in a small space, but can be a concern in a larger lecture theatre. Students who can't even hear what you're saying are going to switch off pretty quickly. At conferences, you can see delegates filling in their diaries and doing the crossword whenever the lecturer with the little voice comes on.

You also need to make sure that you vary the tone and pitch of your voice as you talk; otherwise you could end up boring your students by droning or talking in flat monotones. But communication isn't just about using your voice. There is also body language. Loll around in your chair with your feet on the desk and your students may think that you're either too bored or too lazy to teach them.

A good tutor uses gestures, nods, eye contact and facial expressions to communicate interest to the students. If a student is talking to you, you don't need to keep on repeating 'Yes, that's a good point'; nodding the head from time to time helps get the message over. You also need to make sure that you adapt your language to suit the group. You cannot use the same jargon and specialist vocabulary with beginners as you can with advanced learners.

Communication is also a two-way process. When students speak to you, you have to show that you are listening. For instance, jotting down the main points of what students tell you will help you remember what they have said and will show the students that their points of view are worth noting. You can then use what the student has said as the basis for a clarification, or to restate what they have told you or can summarise the student's main points before moving on to the next stage.

If students are working on individual projects, for instance in a woodworking class, then it's not a bad idea to keep a note of what each of them is working on in a folder.

Arranging the room

One of the most important aspects of how students interact in your group is the physical layout of the room. Of course, you are often restricted as to what you can do. A lecture theatre with tiered seating is not easily rearranged without a good supply of Semtex, although if you have a small group, at least huddling close together is better than directing the lesson to all the corners of the theatre. Likewise computer suites, workshops and other specialist areas are what they are. Gather people around one work-bench if you want to talk to them. Spread them out when you want them to work on a project.

If you do get a chance to set out your room, then there are several possibilities. The following are just a few examples. None of these might suit you. Whichever arrangement you choose, you should bear in mind your teaching style, your subject and the learning activities you are expecting in a particular session. You can soon train weekly students to arrange the room for you; if you are teaching or training on a one-day session, you should arrange the room yourself.

Serried ranks

I'm sure that most of us remember the layout shown in Figure 3.1 from our own schooldays. Your students will probably remember it as well. For some that famil-iarity will be reassuring; for others it will be off-putting.

Although the sightline for the tutor is good, it is not necessarily particularly great for students. Some of them will find it difficult to see what is going on. It is also onerous to get any kind of interaction between students. It's not very pleasant being unable to see the person behind you when they or you are speaking.

The layout shown in Figure 3.2 can be fine for lectures, but it's all too easy to end up talking only to those students who fit in the teaching 'V', ignoring those down the sides of the wing. It is rare to see this kind of seating arrangement in adult education, although if you have fixed or heavy furniture, you may have little option.

Circle

You can easily arrange most rooms to take a circular arrangement of chairs, either with or without tables as shown in Figure 3.3. There are advantages and disadvan-tages to having tables. If you don't use tables, it means that the group can become very intimate. The open circle is fine for open discussions and work in which it is important to break down barriers, such as with counselling. Tables, as well as giving the learner somewhere to write, also form a barrier. Now, a barrier is not necessarily a negative thing to have. It can stop the learner from feeling too vulnerable. It also gives students somewhere to put all their equipment and a surface to write on.

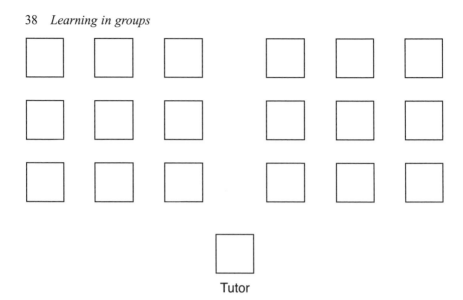

Tutor

Figure 3.1 Serried ranks

A circle can be a very effective way of working, but don't forget that some students like working on their own, so they might find this particular layout a little distracting. One variation that students seem to hate in the extreme (and I share their odium) is those tables that have a little built-in swinging platform onto which you can only just get a piece of A4 paper. I realise that they're often used as a compromise solution to save space, but they seem neither fish, nor fowl, nor red herring. Besides, if you've got anybody left-handed in your group, the chances are that they can never find the left-handed version of the chair or they end up writing across their own bodies.

Groups of tables

The layout shown in Figure 3.4 works particularly well if you want your students to work in small groups. You generally need a good-sized room to do it, and it means that you can circulate quickly between groups.

It is not particularly effective if you are going to give lots of formal input. Some students will have to strain and crane to see you or the board. It also means that it is very easy for students to carry on side conversations when you want them to focus on you.

Where this set-up works particularly well is if you are frequently moving back-and-forth between plenary and small groups.

Oblongs

There are two essential variations of the oblong. One is the 'chairman of the board'-style layout, where you can group tables into an oblong, or use one large

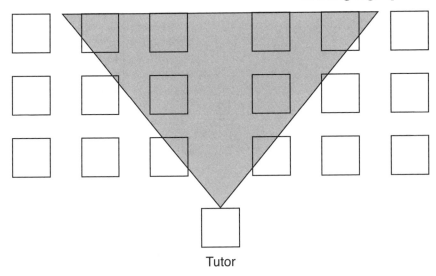

Tutor

Figure 3.2 Teaching in the V

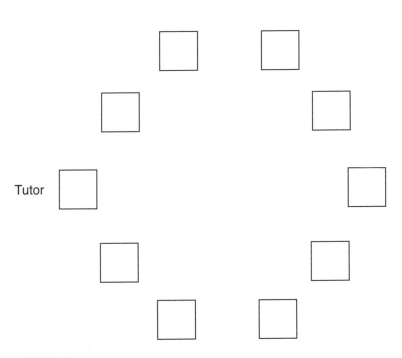

Figure 3.3 Circle

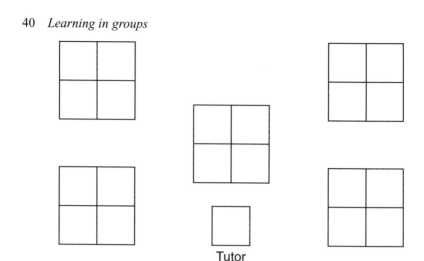

Tutor

Figure 3.4 Groups of tables

conference-style table, and sit around it. As a tutor, you can see most students, although you may find that some have to stretch a little to see you and you must-n't overlook those sitting closest to you. This layout is excellent with small groups, and if your students are dealing with a lot of paperwork, then they have plenty of room to spread out.

The 'open oblong' shown in Figure 3.5 is the same kind of idea, but leaves the teacher's end of the oblong open. Its advantage over the 'chairman of the board' is that you can circulate inside the oblong, giving attention to both individual and clus-ters of students. It also doesn't take a lot of furniture moving to break the group into pairs or small groups. As I tend to teach subjects where people need to spread out their paperwork and often divide the group into pairs and smaller groups, it works well for me. However, I do usually have the luxury of groups limited to around 12 students. If you start to get more than this, then you need a big room to cope with this layout.

To sum up

Teaching a group, composed of very different individuals, is no easy business. It takes a lot of skill and practice. Most jobs and professions require dealing with people on an individual basis. Doctors are never asked to diagnose eye problems, gastro-enteritis, athlete's foot, impetigo and hay fever from amongst a group of 20 people all at the same time. Nor are dentists expected to perform multiple-drilling or plumbers to unblock 16 toilets simultaneously. You will be expected to do the educational equivalent. It's a tough job, but enormously rewarding when you do it well.

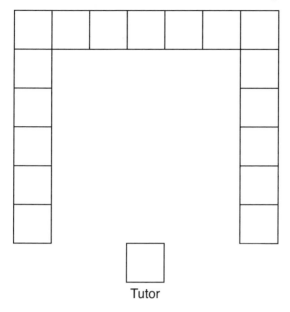

Tutor

Figure 3.5 The open oblong

As the tutor, it is your responsibility to create an effective learning group. You should do so by:

- ensuring that your management style encourages student participation
- dealing promptly and effectively with potential disruptions
- ensuring that your communication style is right for the group
- dealing sympathetically with your students
- making sure that your room is as comfortable as it can be
- setting out your room to make learning as effective as possible
- creating the right atmosphere in the class
- showing your students that you care about their opinions and ideas
- valuing your students as individuals
- having a sense of humour and proportion.

We can't be brilliant teachers all the time. If our students know that, despite our shortcomings, we have their best interests at heart, they will respect what we are doing for them. Teaching is not a popularity contest though it is not enough just to appear like a 'nice lady' or a 'decent cove'. You have to use a range of methods to enable your students to learn. In the next chapter we'll have a look at some of the methods that you and your students can use and discuss their uses and abuses, advantages and disadvantages, dangers and glories.

4   Teaching and learning methods

No matter how new you are to teaching, you will have come across many of the methods in this chapter. You may not know what they are called and you may come across them wearing slightly different names and disguises, but they will be familiar all the same. The techniques described here are not meant to form an exhaustive list, but it should give you an idea of some of the methods available to you.

We can divide teaching methods into two general categories – teacher-centred methods and learner-centred methods. With teacher-centred methods, the teacher tends to play the part of the circus ringmaster. Everything that takes place in the classroom is heavily directed by the tutor. With learner-centred methods, it is the learner who is allowed to take greater personal charge over his or her own learning.

For example, the traditional method of teaching older students is the lecture. The lecture is a way in which one person can give information to a large group, generally without any form of interruption. In a lecture, it is the teacher who has control over the amount and level of information students are exposed to. Other types of teacher-centred activities include demonstrations, talks, lecturettes and tutor-led discussions.

Teacher-centred methods are fine, no matter what anyone tells you. Where they can become a problem is when they are the only method you employ. If you're not careful, it can become extremely tedious for your students. You end up talking far too much and, frankly, it's very hard work for you.

There is an old adage amongst teachers 'teacher talk – five per cent effective; student do – 95 per cent effective'. There's a lot of truth in this. If you find yourself thinking 'I've told my students this a million times, why don't they listen', remind yourself that talking at/to students for any length of time inevitably leads them to bouts of narcolepsy.

At the other end of the spectrum is, of course, learner-centred education. You may also find it called 'student-centred' learning – it's exactly the same thing. As its name suggests, it puts the learner and not the teacher at the centre of the activity. Study tours, discovery learning, distance learning, buzz groups and brainstorming are typical examples of this kind of approach. Good teachers use this kind of learning as a way of allowing their students the freedom to do their own work at their own pace and to discover things for themselves. Bad teachers use it as an excuse not to do any teaching and abdicate responsibility for their students' progress. The danger is that without any direction, student-centred learning can become flabby. Small group and individual work need clearly stated aims. Yet again, the idea of having a partnership with your students is crucial. You must co-operate and collaborate to enable them to get the best of all possible methods.

Mix and match

We've already seen how your students are a mixed bunch with different learning preferences. They may find some activities tedious or simply inappropriate. You need to mix the activities that take place in your classroom and match them to what you are trying to teach.

Not all the methods listed here will be useful for your subject. There is probably no 'right' method for teaching anything. Beware of the Shamans who sell one-size-fits-all educational solutions. You must make decisions on which methods you use based on your skills and aptitudes and the students' inclinations, abilities and previous knowledge. Most teachers have a tendency to rely on a few stock methods and to ignore others. Try to keep an open mind as you read through and think how you might use the methods for your subject.

Good teachers will try to use as many different teaching techniques as they can in order to give their students good lessons. They also like their students to develop into autonomous learners. If you can help to develop good study habits in your students, it will equip them for other subjects in the future.

Teacher-centred methods

Lecture and lecturette

The old-fashioned lecture is the most direct method of transferring knowledge from one person to a large group. The lecture is much maligned as a means of teaching, mainly because we have all suffered such appalling periods of unmitigated tedium at the hands of lecturers who have done for teaching what the Boston strangler did for door-to-door selling.

It is the method that is at the core of most University teaching. I conducted a quick, small, completely unscientific survey of my current young undergraduate class – or to put it in real terms, I chatted with them about lectures over coffee. Not one of my group of 20+ managed anything more positive than a neutral comment. Some of their replies were so coruscating that they are too strong to be seen in print. Above all, most of them liked classes in which there was a mix of activities.

It's easy when you're an old cynic to dismiss this as simply the moaning of a generation whose attention span has been atomised by fast-edited television shows with hand-held cameras and jump-cuts, and the advent of the remote control. Most of my university mates, a generation earlier thought lectures pretty dull too and we only had three plodding channels and had to get out of our chairs to turn the television over. I suspect that it has always been thus. When I give those same students a well-thought-out task that absorbs and challenges them, they will concentrate for ages.

Unless you are a spellbinding speaker of huge personal wit, wisdom and knowledge, use the lecture sparingly. If there are some topics or areas of your course which you think would best be dealt with in a lecture, try to keep it as short as you can and, if possible, make it more of a lecturette (same thing, but shorter). Unless your group is enormous, ensure that you can be interrupted when a point needs clarification. Similarly, if you can break up the lecture by other forms of student involvement, do. You're lecturing on the future of print journalism – why not see if your students can guess which newspapers sell the most copies. A lecture about a trip across America? Give them a hand-out with some of the places marked, so they can follow it and add their own notes. Look in the next chapter on resources that are available to teachers and students for ideas as to how to present some of your lecture visually, add impact, or simply break up the one-way traffic that is the lecture.

If you do lecture, always allow some time for a question-and-answer activity or a discussion at some point in the session, otherwise the ideas you have been trying to get across will soon be lost. Many tutors new to teaching feel that if they are not 'doing the work' all the time, they are not giving value for money.

At the end of a lecture, lecturers have a tendency to ask their audience, 'Has anyone any questions?' If they are met by a wall of silence, either they have given such a blindingly good lecture that every possible point has been covered, or they have simply bored the audience into stunned silence. It's much better to pose a few questions asking students for their opinions about any individual points you have covered or to show what they have learned in some practical way – perhaps through a demonstration or some kind of written exercise. I will cover testing and assessment more thoroughly in Chapter 7, but if you are preparing a lecture, don't forget to include a list of questions for any post-lecture discussion. Treat it as an essential part of the lecture.

If you find a lecture is a sandwich with no filling, then you could try the lecture's little sister, the lecturette. Essentially it is the same as a lecture, but smaller – obvious, really!

The lecturette is a more useful method than the full blown lecture for three main reasons. First, it allows more time in the session for a variety of other teaching methods so your session can appeal to more learners. Second, you won't end up staring at rows of dulled, grey faces politely (if you are lucky) stifling yawns and looking surreptitiously at their watches. Third, it enables you to move from individual or small group activities back to focus on a topic as a larger group. I'm actually a big fan of the lecturette for the kinds of subjects that I teach which are usually based around education, the social sciences or creative writing. For instance, if you were teaching about the laws of libel, you could use the lecturette to explain the general principles, and then divide your students into smaller groups for them to look at a particular case study.

For both lectures and lecturettes, it can be worthwhile preparing a handout of the main points, so that students can follow your lecture and jot down their own reactions in some logical sequence, although there is a danger that students don't learn how to devise their own overall note-taking techniques.

Explanation

It seems almost silly to mention this one, but experts often forget how difficult some things can be for the beginner. Explanations could be to the whole group 'I will explain how a nuclear reactor works', or could be on an individual or small group basis. It is especially useful to help clarify a point. Students often ask for individual clarifications. This means that you have to be quick at thinking of different ways of explaining the same material.

Explanations should be clear and concise. Encouraging students to give their own explanations of what you cover in class is often a good technique for allowing them to consolidate knowledge. You will also often be surprised by how many students learn a great deal from other students' little 'side explanations'. You may not be the only teacher in the class!

Talks and presentations

'Talk' is the term often used for informal lectures that are laid on by such groups as the Women's Institute, University of the Third Age and hobbyist organisations. You often see them advertised at the local shop on topics such as local history, travel or personal experience. Think of the talk as being a light-hearted lecture, best with a few touches of humour, which works well if you can get in a few anecdotes. Often, a talk will be illustrated in some way, perhaps with slides. This can be a much more interesting way of passing on your knowledge than the straightforward stand-and-spout-till-they-fall-asleep technique.

Presentation tends to be the term that is commonly used in commercial and organisational settings for what is essentially a talk. Again, it's another variation on the lecture-lecturette-demonstration style of teaching. Remember, you are probably talking to extremely busy people who have other commitments. Keep to the schedule and don't over-run.

Demonstration

Hobbyist organisations might also include demonstrations on their calendars. Demonstrations are very often used in skill-based subjects, such as arts and crafts. It's a practical version of a lecture. As with the lecture, there is nothing wrong with demonstration, but you should avoid certain traps. First is the 'And here's one I made earlier' trap, where the tutor, having gone through a series of very complicated tasks, whips out a brilliantly-executed example, leaving the students totally demoralised because they got lost at stage two. Second, a skills-based subject is to do with learning skills – the name is a bit of a give-away. But it is very easy to end up demonstrating all the time and not allowing your students to get their hands dirty. Lecturing someone on how to wire a plug is not nearly as useful as demonstrating how to do it. However, if the students don't get to wire their own plugs, then you've wasted their time.

If you teach a craft subject and find yourself circulating around the class dispensing help, the demonstration comes in handy in two different ways. Instead of jumping in to do the task in hand for the individual student, demonstrate what they need to do and allow them to do it for themselves – they will learn so much more, even if they don't get it quite right to begin with. Also, it is worth getting either the whole group or a small group together in order to demonstrate one particular, or a small series of skills.

Another technique is to demonstrate the activity with the class actually doing it at the same time. You can see this type of activity frequently in physical exercise classes, but it could equally be used for boning a leg of lamb or showing students how to tie knots, connect copper pipes, plant seedlings or operate a piece of machinery.

Good practice for lecturing, demonstrating and presenting

I reiterate that there is nothing wrong with a presentational style of teaching, but you must bear in mind what makes for good practice and the pitfalls to avoid.

Prepare thoroughly

Just because you know your subject, this doesn't mean that you don't have to plan what you are going to do – make sure that you decide exactly what your students need to know.

Emphasise key points

Make sure that the key points are obvious. Use bullet-points or little summaries to help the learner.

Speak up

Make sure you can be heard. We were convinced at university that our lecturers had all grown beards just so they could mumble into them – even the women. Your voice should be clear and loud.

Don't bore your audience

A touch of humour is great, as is the occasional anecdote or illustrative story. But if your lecture turns into a stand-up comedy routine, then some students may feel that they haven't got what they paid for. It's easy to try to be too entertaining, often because you are nervous and think that a joke or two will go down well.

Know your audience

This is a tough one, especially if you're giving a one-off talk to a group of people you've never met before. If you can reasonably expect that the learners will know the technical terms for your subject, use them. They will feel talked down to if you don't. On the other hand, if you pepper a talk to a more general audience with jargon they cannot possibly know, then they too are going to switch off.

Learner comfort

Make sure the learners are comfortable, but not so comfortable that they doze off. Often you have little control over this, but you can at least make sure windows are open on stuffy days.

Punctuality

Keep to time. Your learners may well need to be somewhere else. Leave enough time for questions at the end.

Mannerisms

Mannerisms – whether quirks of speech or physical ones – can be off-putting if your learners begin to concentrate on them, rather than what you are saying. We all have tics and habits and it is difficult to keep them under control. Make sure that you, and what you have to say, outshine those minor eccentricities.

A mate of mine, often called upon to do company presentations, has been drilled into keeping his arms by his sides so that the audience doesn't follow his waving hands. I think this is taking it a bit far. Gestures can help enliven what you have to say. Just don't go overboard. Similarly, the 'errs', 'aahs' and 'umms' of everyday speech can get in the way of what you are trying to say – again, these are furiously difficult to control.

Your learners will forgive you many of these habits, if you talk enthusiastically and knowledgeably about your subject.

Questioning and quizzes

Often at the end of a more teacher-centred process, there will be a period of questioning. This can be the opportunity for learners to ask for clarifications or opinions or further information.

You can also ask questions. It's tempting to see questioning purely as a way of testing students' knowledge (see Chapter 6 – Assessment and evaluation). True, we use questions in order to check understanding and awareness or to make sure that we have explained something as well as we can, but you can use questions as a very powerful teaching tool. They can certainly encourage your students to think more deeply about a subject.

We tend to mix in similar social circles or to read one kind of newspaper. We can become very set in our views and our opinions. Teachers and academics are amongst the worst at this, grabbing our copies of the Guardian as we tut-tut at the state of the world. If we ask our students questions that mean they have to look into other sets of views and opinions, we are educating them. We are not telling them that their opinions are wrong, but we are opening up the world to them. We too can be wrong.

When you look at an exercise, a passage or a section of a textbook, make a list of questions that will provoke your students into thinking more. What are the pertinent questions? What are some easy ones to get you started? What would the devil's advocate ask?

You can also use quizzes both as a means of testing existing knowledge and as a means of light-hearted revision. Again, individuals do not necessarily like being put on the spot, but if you use the pub quiz technique, whereby you have small teams and the answers are written down, then you won't put them 'on the spot' too much. I have seen this technique used to puncture myths, by asking students to answer questions at which they are likely only to be able to guess the answer – how much CO_2 does a certain marque of car emit? How much does an author earn when her book is taken out of a library? Which profession has the highest suicide rate?

Students often like this kind of semi-competition, although some can be put off. Again, if you make it seem like a light-hearted piece of fun, then that is how the students will perceive it. If you have the odd student who likes to coast a bit, admittedly they can get away with the minimum amount of work, but it also gives the shyer, more knowledgeable students a chance to show what they can do without their having to do it in front of a large group. It is also a good technique for a new tutor to use, as you can still feel 'in charge' of the session, but at the same time, you are allowing the students to do most of the work.

Above all, think of questioning as a teaching technique as well as a means of testing. It really can be a powerful teaching tool.

Questioning techniques

We will look at questioning as a means of assessment in Chapter 6. Although there is some overlap with using questions as a teaching technique, the two are not entirely the same.

There are largely two types of question – the open question and the closed question.

A closed question normally requires a simple 'yes/no' answer, or a straightforward fact. 'Is the Pope Catholic?' is a closed question, as is 'What was the date of the Battle of Waterloo?' It is, for instance, useful for testing basic understanding, great in foreign language classes, or craft classes where a certain formula needs to be followed to achieve the desired result. You can always disguise the closed question with this kind of variation – 'Can anyone tell me which muscles we work when we do sit-ups?'

On the other hand, a question such as 'Do you think we should remain in NATO?' is an open question. It is asking for a point-of-view, an explanation or an opinion. Questions such as these are great for exploring theme-based topics and for encouraging students to develop their own ideas and opinions. Liberal arts, the social sciences and creative subjects (amongst others) cry out for the use of the open question.

Don't fall into the trap of asking too general an open question. For example, if you show students a film and then ask 'what did you think of that?', you might find that you get a poor response. It may be that you've cast your net far too wide and the silence with which you are greeted is not that your students don't care, it's just that they don't know where to start. A question, such as 'Did you like the ending' or 'Which bit did you like best', followed by a swift 'Why?' narrows the focus and yet still asks for opinions.

One of the dangers of questioning is to fall into the trap of asking 'guess what I'm thinking' questions. 'What is the most important aspect of Christianity?' might lead to a rigorous discussion. On the other hand, students might sit there in total bewilderment, wondering if there is an actual answer to the question, just as they did after you showed them the film a paragraph or two ago.

Question and answer (Q&A) is not the same as discussion. Q&A tends to be more teacher-directed. Discussion allows students to interact with each other much more. It is fairly common to find that you end up with something of a hybrid of the two, using a bit of Q&A to lead into a discussion.

Debates and panels

Debates may seem a bit old-fashioned now, but what's wrong in that? Sometimes old-fashioned techniques are so different for a younger generation, that they have a novelty value. A debate uses a statement as its opening gambit, usually in the form of 'This house believes that the prison system is ineffective'.

Normally, the debate is guided by a chairperson. You have two people to represent each side of the argument, taking it in turns to do so – pro-con, pro-con. After they have presented their arguments, the audience is allowed to ask them questions. Once all the questions have been answered, the audience (the house) should then vote for the side that has put forward the more persuasive argument.

In an era when emotions seem more important than analysis, it is sometimes difficult for people to leave their own personal opinions out of their decisions. They should, in theory, be voting for the best-constructed argument. In practice, they have a tendency to vote for whoever they sided with before the debate began.

Don't forget that some students might feel singled out if they were expected to stand up and give a formal talk. Also, the students who are not going to speak formally may need guidance in order to think about the kinds of questions they might like to ask. You might also wonder what the students who are listening are actually doing.

This is not a method you would want to use every lesson, but fun once a year for some subjects. It might even be worth getting in a couple of outside 'experts'.

Debates can be a useful learning method for subjects where the ability to express an argument or a point of view is part of the subject. It also exposes the students to different points of view and ideas that they might not otherwise have considered. Debates are often used in English, the social sciences and study skills courses.

Panel

Perhaps less daunting for students than standing up to take part in a debate is a panel. This method can work very well; think of all the examples on the radio or television, such as Gardeners' Question Time or Any Questions. Weekend news programmes also often have a gentler version of this, where columnists, journalists and politicians are asked to give their views on the preceding week and the way it has been reported.

In the classroom, you can use either a small group of expert outsiders, or members of the group who are well-informed on a certain topic or topics, or who have worked on a specific area for the occasion and are then expected to answer questions from the group.

The main danger is with the person (either 'panellist' or 'audience') whose real specialism is pontificating about absolutely nothing.

I once saw an excellent drama lesson, which used a version of the panel. One group of students gave a rehearsed reading of a play. At the end of the reading, they stayed in character whilst other students asked them questions about the play and their feelings. This was a brilliant exercise. The 'acting' students not only developed their skills in performance-style reading, but they also had to work at improvisation. The 'audience' students, not only got to see and hear an extract from a play, but they were able to find out more about each of the characters.

Outside experts and interviews

Students often love the chance to interview an outside expert, especially if they're something of a local celebrity. You might be surprised at how generous some well-known figures can be with their time if it is for an educational project. Others, of course, may demand enormous fees. Approach them with the idea that they would be doing you a huge favour. If your expert has written a book or even several books on the subject in question, you can always encourage them to bring along some copies and mention to your students that they might like to buy some books, because X has so generously given of their time.

Brief the expert fully. Give them the kind of information that they need to know about your group. Tell them something about the group's knowledge, ability, experience and the work you have done to date. Also, make sure that the expert knows exactly what you want from them.

Think about some of the questions that your group might ask. It seems a terrible shame to get in an expert only to find that the Q&A session that you expected to be so vibrant is met with slack-jawed silence.

Interviews can work both with expert outsiders and members of the group. The technique is not just limited to interview practice, for example with a group of unemployed looking for work, but also as a means of getting information from students without putting them under the strain of standing up and giving a talk.

Learner-centred methods

If those are some of the more teacher-centred methods, what is available to place the student at the centre of their own learning? Of course, there is always going to be some overlap between the two (vague) categories of methods, but the following at least emphasise the learner's role in the class, rather than that of the teacher.

Simulation

Simulation is, as its name suggests, a way in which we try to replicate real-life situations in the classroom. The ultimate simulation, of course, is to pilot a moon landing from the safety of a mock-up capsule anchored firmly to the earth. Unfortunately, not every educational establishment has one of these, although many Further Education Colleges have training restaurants, where students can practise and develop their skills in a real-life situation. Fire stations have towers where fire officers can rehearse saving people from burning buildings.

If you were training would-be mountaineers for an Everest expedition, for instance, you could give your students the experience of climbing a smaller mountain here at home. If you use simulation, you must make sure that it is as near the real experience as you can possibly make it, without placing your students at unnecessary risk.

Simulation is not restricted merely to the most adventurous pursuits. Asking students to write and mock-up a newspaper is a form of simulation. In business Studies or financial subjects, creating and following the fortunes of an imaginary investment portfolio would also be a kind of simulation.

Role-play

This technique is a variation on the idea of simulation where members of the group act out a scene, a scenario or a series of parts and then analyse the experience afterwards. Role-plays are often used in the kinds of subjects where we need to explore emotions. Counselling courses and classes involving the practical application of psychology often use role-play. Being lectured how to counsel someone who has just lost their partner is not quite the same as actually going through the motions in a role-play. Often in these situations, the other students are asked to observe what is taking place.

You may also find that some students do not want to role-play in front of the whole group. They might find it awkward or embarrassing. In this case, you might consider using several unobserved role-plays, making the activity seem a little more like pair-work.

Role-plays don't always have to involve complex situations that place an emphasis on affective learning. They can be extremely useful for training people for commercial purposes. For example: How is the receptionist going to deal with an angry customer? How is the tourist on holiday in the Algarve going to buy a loaf of bread, using Portuguese?

Role-plays can be fun and effective, but they need a well-thought-out scenario if they are to work properly. You need to give your students clear instructions as to the parameters of the role-play and what exactly they are trying to simulate.

Games

You can also use games to help with learning. Often, existing board games can be adapted to suit your needs. Scrabble or Boggle, for instance, adapted according to the situation, can be excellent for Basic Skills or language courses. Games add a competitive element to your class. Normally, this is not particularly serious competition, but there is little point in playing a game if you are not intending to win.

I tend to think that dividing a class into smaller groups that then form 'teams' is the safest way of introducing competition. It doesn't put individuals on the spot; it increases teamwork and generally makes for a fun level of competition.

Discovery learning

As we go about our daily lives, we pick up bits and pieces of information and ideas, almost without concentrating. In the modern, information-based age, we can't help it. We're bombarded from all sides with information that slips in under our defences through our ears, eyes, mouths and noses. We soon recognise the smell of fresh-baked bread or the taste of real coffee. We tune in to TV sets and radios, absorb music, news, films, videos. The knowledge, perceptions and skills that we thus accrete are all part of the process of discovery learning.

Some topics lend themselves very well to discovery. Imagine that you are teaching the very subject of this book – adult education. You could ask your students to use the internet to find organisations relevant to adult education and what their functions are, thereby compiling a kind of critical listing. I'm certain that knowledge gained in this way is excellent as students then have a sense of pride and ownership in what they have learnt.

Where discovery learning is truly useful in adult education is the fact that adults, having lived longer than children, have discovered more things and consequently learnt more. This prior experience and learning can sometimes be certificated nowadays (what can't?), but the important thing is that it means that you have a group of students who already know something about your subject and also have general knowledge from the world they inhabit.

On the other hand, asking them to go away and discover the perfect tense of German irregular verbs is a cheat. In this instance, you need to be using other methods – explanations, examples and practice exercises to help the students understand and use the new element of language. This is pure dereliction of duty as a tutor.

Experiential learning

Experiential learning is not quite the same as discovery learning. Experiential learning involves finding out about something by going through the process itself. It's rather like simulation (in fact, what's in a name?). For example, I once went on a course on the way in which groups work. For several days we sat around and discussed how we thought groups worked and, in the end, we discovered whether or not we, as a group, had gone through the processes of forming a group.

For some people, this learning by doing works very well. Alas, though it may be a good technique for those of us who tend towards the pragmatic, as tutors we're often bound by time restrictions on our courses, so this is not necessarily the most time-efficient way to learn something. Quite frankly, I could have read up on what I learned about groups in about half an hour, but it was quite fun watching people determined to humiliate themselves in front of perfect strangers. I must have learnt something, because I got a certificate.

Facilitation

Experiential learning is often facilitated rather than taught. The problem seems to be that no one can quite define 'facilitation', and it means different things depending on which side of the Atlantic you happen to be. Advocates of facilitation will probably send out a lynch mob for my definition (once they've discussed who is going to carry the noose and voted on it democratically), but I think that, in the general context of the teaching of adults, facilitation is to do with allowing students to concentrate on their own learning and you take a step back as a teacher.

If your class has divided into groups and these groups are now working on a problem-solving exercise, when you wander round the class as a resource for the students, then you are teaching in a facilitative way. Facilitation can also be used to describe the process of acting as the chairperson of a group, enabling the group to achieve its aims.

I have a problem with the word itself, which is clumsy and looks as though it should be wearing sandals and eating organic alfalfa sprouts.

Tutorials

If you are working in the further or higher education sectors, you might well be expected to take tutorials. Tutorials are normally either one-to-one sessions with individual students, or with small groups of up to half-a-dozen, although none of this is set in stone. A well-run tutorial will give the tutor and student a two-way process that enables each to feed back to the other.

In the main, there are few tutorials in adult education, although you might think of your little promenades round the room, as people are working, as an opportunity for some kind of mini-tutorial.

If you have to give slightly more formalised tutorials, make sure that you set out an agenda for you and your student. This doesn't have to be the kind of formal agenda you need for a meeting, but you could simply start by saying 'Today, I'd like to discuss the following three things ... have you got anything else you'd like to talk about?' Then, try to stick to the points agreed, otherwise you will find that you end up with a meaningless hodgepodge of chit-chat.

One small caveat here. Occasionally, you read or hear about serious complaints, such as sexual harassment, being made by students about tutors. Some of these will be true – the profession has its villains as does any other; some will be purely vexatious; some may arise from a misunderstanding over a gesture. If I'm meeting a student on a one-to-one basis, I try to do it somewhere informal, such as a coffee bar or a communal area, or do a mini-tutorial within the class itself. Use your common sense and you won't go far wrong.

Brainstorming, buzz groups and snowballing

Even if you've not heard these terms before the chances are that you have used one or other of these methods. The word 'brainstorming' is currently seen as politically incorrect in some quarters, because it could be deemed as offensive to someone with epilepsy. They proffer the alternative of 'word-shower', which sounds like some form of sexual deviancy. I asked a friend with epilepsy if he objected to the word 'brainstorm' and he couldn't think why he should. It's also ingrained with me, so I will use it, even if with some minor reservations.

Brainstorming is a way of listing all the ideas associated with a particular topic, each member of the group contributing randomly. One member of the group (not necessarily the tutor) usually writes the words on a board or a flipchart. This must be done without additional comment from you or the group and all contributions should be recorded without the contributions being altered in any way. The principle behind the technique being that you are encouraging creativity rather than critical thinking.

It is best to keep the period of brainstorming quite short. It can then be followed up with group discussion on the ideas, which have been listed – the critical thinking absent whilst getting words on paper. It is a powerful tool if used well, but can be difficult to manage as a whole group exercise.

You might feel more comfortable trying a variation of brainstorming known as a buzz group, where the class is normally divided into very small groups who think very quickly of ideas associated with a certain topic. Unlike brainstorming, comment is allowed. It is a very useful technique for solving problems or for getting groups to think in a highly creative way. A problem is worked out individually, then students get into pairs to discuss what they have been working on; the process of comparison is taken a step further by working in a four. The groups of four then report back to the whole group.

I'm not the only teacher who finds using brainstorming difficult to control. As I like to promote discussions in my groups, I often find that students want to comment on ideas, which goes against the whole spirit and principle of brainstorming. I have to confess that I always want to get my two pennyworth in as well. As a result, I often end up with a bit of a hybrid.

It is worth trying both methods as they can be very useful learning aids and a good way of ensuring that your group mixes freely.

Case study and problem solving

A case study is simply a grand way of referring to the story of an event, set of circumstances, problem or even a person. The group analyses the case study in order to give possible solutions. For example, you are teaching business studies and looking at how small enterprises can begin exporting to Europe. You might present your group with the histories of two different companies – one of which was successful, the other not. You would then ask students to work out why they thought the business succeeded (or failed).

It is best if a case study is true or at least has the ring of truth. In other words, even if it didn't happen, it might well have done. This is vital in pragmatic subjects, where if you're not too careful it can all sound like theory. Case studies allow you to make your own hypotheses, test them out and look at solutions.

Some problems lend themselves best to individual solution (too many cooks spoil the broth). Other problems are best dealt with in groups, where you often find that the range of ideas generated is much greater and much more creative. It is for you to decide what works best on the merit of each problem.

Flexible learning, open learning and distance learning

If you are teaching in traditional mainstream adult education (what is currently referred to as Adult and Community Learning), with its borrowed classrooms and equipment, you are probably unlikely to come across these types of learning. In colleges, Higher Education, commerce and industry, however, they have become very popular ways of teaching students.

Open learning is a blanket term to cover all the sorts of learning which takes place largely on an individual basis with the learner working at his or her own pace, usually at home or in the workplace, and where the student has very little contact with the tutor. Open learning covers home learning, distance learning, correspondence courses, etc.

You may find that some of your students are studying an open learning course in the same, or a similar subject, elsewhere and are using your class as a kind of support mechanism, but for the traditional adult education tutor, these kinds of methods of learning are not normally used in a formal sense, but you may find yourself doing so as and when necessary. Many adult education tutors give out their own telephone numbers or email addresses so that their students can contact them as and when necessary. I have found that it is rare that students take advantage of the tutor by telephoning at all hours of the day and night. Contact by phone and email is one way in which you are providing a little additional service – a safety net, a mini-tutorial, a guiding or helping hand – to students who do not have the full formal back-up that larger educational establishments might be able to provide.

As with many of the topics in this book, teaching via the internet deserves an entire book to itself. The internet has opened up a whole range of courses that make learning available to anyone with access to a computer, meaning that potential students are not limited by being housebound, living in some remote area or with awkward domestic or work patterns. As fees increase and part-time courses become widely available for greater numbers of the population, learning via the web is revving up and ready to accelerate. It is also a means by which the teaching of minority interest subjects can be assured.

Surprisingly, it is both more time-consuming and more difficult to run an internet-based course than it is to run a conventional class. Whilst teaching via the internet looks like a means of earning money without leaving the house, it is not a soft option.

The difficulty with teaching via the internet is that you are missing parts of communication that most of us take for granted – sight and hearing. In a classroom, there is eye contact, the little nod of the head to show you're listening, the smile of encouragement for the nervous student, the warm tone in your voice welcoming the group. On the internet, there's just the intense glare of the screen.

If you hand back an excellent piece of work that has got maximum marks with the quip 'that was terrible – you should be ashamed of yourself', the student will know you are pulling their leg the moment they see the high marks for the work. Write the same thing in an on-line conference and the student may not see the irony. What was a joke (admittedly not a good one), could turn into the most crushing blow, when you had no such intention. Misunderstandings can be frequent. If one student writes in capital letters on a conference, the other students see it as shouting; even if the reality is that the poor chap has simply accidentally hit the caps lock key and doesn't know how to undo it.

You may also find that there is a mismatch of language between some students. Younger students, used to the abbreviations and acronyms of texting, may use a code that seems incomprehensible to older students. I once thought that I was obviously the target of transparent affection from a couple of my on-line students, obviously ready to fight a duel over me, only to find that 'LOL' didn't mean 'lots of love', but 'laugh out loud'. You can't win them all. The average 19-year old can now text a 15,000 word dissertation in 12 minutes flat, using just two thumbs. During that time, I'm still looking for the semi-colon key on a full-sized keyboard. Some students may find texting an 'abomination of the Queen's English'; others may find it useful shorthand.

One of the means to teaching well via the internet seems to be to do everything that you would do normally to create a good class atmosphere, only be more careful about it because of the fragility and ease of misunderstanding that characterises the internet.

Sometimes, you have to nip things in the bud on-line. 'Flame Wars' is the jargon for a situation whereby students' comments skid out of control and become little more than slanging matches. It's not a bad idea to make light of this – also if you're monitoring your on-line discussion forum or conference, you should spot these things before they happen. You can use little smileys, sometimes also known as emoticons. These are punctuation marks that you read by looking at them sideways, thus :-) becomes a smiling face, or you can quite simply stick in the symbol ☺, which does the job. They may be a bit naff, but at least they're a way of conveying lightness of touch.

You will need all the lightness of touch you can muster. Student demands are very high on internet-based courses. We are an increasingly consumer-led society and sometimes students may feel that studying via the internet, they are not getting the 'value-for-money' that they would be getting face-to-face. Also, because the internet is available 24 hours per day, every day of the year, there can be an expectation that you are similarly available. I've had students phone after 10 o'clock at night and, sin of sins, during major fixtures of the sporting calendar. I'm lucky. One distance tutor has had students turn up in the early hours of the morning to hand in their work personally because their computer was misbehaving, ringing the doorbell until the poor woman in question stumbled downstairs in her dressing-gown to answer the door. These students are, of course, the minority. At the other extreme, you get other students who daren't even approach you to ask a question, because they fear they will be disturbing you. The majority are wonderful, warm human beings who are kind to animals.

Don't forget that with all forms of distance learning, the comments and marks you make on any assessment carry even greater importance than they do in a classroom. Sometimes, this is the only method available to you for any kind of dialogue with your students. Be as positive as you can. Rather than talking in terms of 'where you have gone wrong', try to be positive – 'where could you improve'. Many of us, myself included, aren't naturally as good at this as we could be – some of us are natural straight-talkers, others much cleverer at wrapping bad news in cheerful, ribboned parcels. Remind yourself that the raw comments at the end of a piece are even more important for a distance-learning student than they are for the student sitting in your class, who can instantly ask for clarification.

Group discussion

There are two main types of discussion. One is guided discussion where the tutor leads the group through a series of questions to arrive at certain conclusions. In a general group discussion, where the group can consist of all the members of the class or smaller sub-groups, the tutor might take a back seat or join in as an equal member or take on the role of devil's advocate. Essentially it is a freer kind of group, allowing for everyone (in theory) to join in. However, large groups can quickly be dominated by one or two individuals, so it is often worth breaking into smaller groups, so that the meek and the quiet can participate.

One very popular and effective way of teaching subjects where discussion is important, is to have a handout that covers your main points. You can then talk through with your students the items on the handout one by one. This is a great technique for mixing your own formal input and drawing on students' own experience and knowledge. This gives the session a relaxed, but purposeful, atmosphere. Without the handout, it might seem too informal. Students may well feel that 'chat' is for coffee breaks and that you should do 'real work' in class.

Seminar

This is a very controlled form of group discussion. A seminar starts with a paper (by that we mean someone reads out an article or essay they have written) or an introductory lecture by an 'expert' (this could be a student), which has a clearly stated argument. You hope that this argument will then get the group so excited that fruitful discussion will ensue. It needs an excellent speaker/lecturer, preferably one being quite controversial, and some firm leadership at the discussion stage.

However, the word 'seminar' is often used to denote university-type work, where the groups are not enormous – often no more than 15–20. In such academic settings, the main form of teaching is often the lecture, so the seminar provides students with a welcome break and allows you to use a much wider variety of teaching techniques.

Small groups

Dividing your class into smaller groups can work very well. You may find that your students always form the same little groups. This is not necessarily a problem, unless those groups begin to look a little bit cliquey.

Most adult classes are quite happy to break up into different small groups from week-to-week. They are not particularly worried about who they work with. If you do find that individual groups are becoming factions, or you want to avoid this happening, it's not too difficult to come up with a series of little strategies for organising your sub-groups. For instance, you might use register order, or surnames, or draw names from a hat. Don't overdo it. Some people come to adult education to learn together. If a husband and wife are learning about interior design, they may well want to be together so that they can put the skills they learn to use on a joint basis.

Working in groups is a very important aspect of adult learning. Throughout this book I have stressed that adults already know a great deal. Working in small groups allows your students to swap ideas and expertise and to learn from each other. It is also a useful way to encourage friendship and socialisation amongst the members of the group.

Group working is not always straightforward. Occasionally, one group can complete an exercise in a world record time, whilst another struggles along. It's often worth having additional activities up your sleeve for group work, as well as for individual exercises.

Sometimes a sub-group can get a little stuck. It's your responsibility to help unstick them. You need to be ready to give information, to help redirect their thinking or give explanations as appropriate. Try opening with, 'Can I give you any help' rather than, 'You lot look a bit stuck. Could you do with a helping hand?'

Displays

Holding a display is a good method of allowing students to show-off their work and a chance for them to feel proud of their achievements. Don't think of a display merely in terms of a bunch of pictures on a wall.

Art groups can put up their pictures, craft groups can show off their creations. Creative writing groups can publish their poems and stories in little home-made booklets (a booklet of their work is, essentially, a display). Cookery groups can allow other students to taste their dishes.

One residential college where I work encourages the students on different courses to have a wander around the other groups during the coffee break. Positive comments from students doing completely different courses are extremely encouraging. I have yet to see the motor-cycle maintenance class link up with keep-fit group to do human pyramids around the adult education centre car park, but I look forward to it with relish.

The great thing about a display is that it not only allows students to be proud of their achievements, but it also shows potential students what they might achieve. If you are going to hold some kind of display or exhibition, it is also worth seeing it as a chance to involve the local press. They are often looking for a story and your class is an important part of the local fabric.

Project

A project can be undertaken on an individual, small group or whole group basis. Generally it is a larger piece of work than usual, allowing for research by the group or the individual. Projects need a good deal of guidance from the tutor if they are not going to flounder.

In craft classes, students often come with their own projects in mind, such as the woodwork class where one student intended making her own coffin.

Ice-breakers and warm-ups

An ice-breaker is a game or short activity aimed at allowing you and the group to get to know each other at the start of a course. Ice-breakers can also be used as warm-up activities at the start of a session. One typical ice-breaker is when the group stands in a circle and throws a soft ball or a bean bag to one another. The person doing the throwing has to name the person who is to catch the ball. Of course, this calls for a little bit of manual dexterity, and we're not all blessed with that!

One ice-breaker that can be used in a variety of forms is the 'Find someone who...'. Students need a sheet of paper on which they have a series of commands, such as 'Find someone who has travelled more than ten miles to be here today' or 'Find someone who has a red car'. It simply gets them talking to each other.

Warm-ups are similar, but have the intention of restarting a group, rather than getting them going in the first place. You are more likely to need these in the early stages of teaching a group that meets on a regular basis, rather than on a short, or intensive course.

Even cleverer are warm-ups that are in themselves educational and relevant to what you are teaching. For instance, if you are teaching a course for students wanting to write a family or personal history, you could get them to circulate and find out from each student something exciting that has happened to them or their family, which they might like to write about. Then, as well as being an excuse for some general chit-chat, it provides a possible entrée to a full-blown exercise.

Marking work or assignments

Often, assessment seems like something that is tacked onto a course. In fact, it is an important tool in the teaching armoury. Whilst I discuss assessment and evaluation more fully in Chapter 6, and have already mentioned it in connection with distance learning, it's worth taking a brief look at 'marking' as a teaching and learning method.

Put yourself back in the shoes of that Business Studies teacher of a couple of pages ago for a moment. You've set a class-based exercise looking at a couple of case studies. Let's say, that for the students' assessed work they have to hand you a 1,000-word report entitled 'Advice for small businesses exporting to Europe'. If you simply stick a few ticks here and there and scrawl '17/20,very good' in red ink, you've done your student a disservice. You don't have to write reams, but how about something useful? Tell the student what they've done well, tell them what they could have done better and tell them what they could do next time to improve their marks. If you've got a small enough group you can feed back individually whilst the group is doing an exercise. However, if you do nothing, then the opportunity to help the student make progress is lost.

Even on an informal level, feeding back to students about their work is a vital part of the teacher's role, which we will explore more fully later.

Field trips

Field trips and study tours are an excellent way of getting outside the classroom and visiting places of interest to the group. The Art class can go to a gallery; the French class on a day trip to Boulogne (if you're close enough). Field trips are a good means of bringing a subject to life.

However, beware of turning an educational trip into something that can be booked through a travel agent. A good field trip will involve preparation and planning. Will you need to hire a coach or a minibus? Can students find their way themselves? Can you negotiate some kind of group discount? Don't forget, there may be students for whom the cost of an educational trip is prohibitive. You need to find out if there is any way in which you can help pay for their costs, without embarrassing them. You also need to prepare the students for the educational aspect of the trip.

So, if you are going to the art gallery, try to visit it yourself beforehand, or if it is too far away, get hold of a catalogue. You can then prepare useful tasks for your students to do. You might, for instance, prepare a worksheet that identifies certain works of art that illustrate different artist's techniques.

Once you've got all this educational stuff out of the way, then you can open the crate of lager on the back seat and get busy with the community singing.

And finally

Choosing appropriate methods and a variety of them is vital in constructing positive, useful sessions where learning actually takes place. A good mixed bag of teacher- and learner-centred techniques always works well, especially if you match technique to content. There's little point in role-playing how to strip an engine, you may as well strip one.

The worst example of failing to match technique to content I've ever witnessed was a lecture entitled something like 'Using student-centred techniques to enhance the individual learning experience'. Not only was the title pompous – it should have been something like 'learner-centred activities'. Worse still, the lecture, which seemed to last longer than the build-up to the US presidential elections, involved a gentleman in a fly-specked blazer, head buried in a sheaf of papers who mumbled about the importance of engaging the students in activities pertinent to their needs. He failed with me. Right then, my need was to be elsewhere.

Your students will, after a while, be happy to become involved in deciding which methods will be most appropriate for your course. To begin with you might get the 'you're the teacher' reply, which may indicate that you should be getting on with the job, but is probably likelier to be because they feel they don't have a right to say what goes on in the class. Of course they do. If they don't like discussing this in class time, grab them over coffee or when they're working individually or in small groups. Ask them if they have any particular preference for the various methods you use. Feedback from students is as important for the methods you use as it is for the content of your course. Even if they can't see it to begin with, your students will soon come to value the fact that you are so open to ideas.

We've seen that at one end of the scale there is the lecture, where the teacher has to do all the real work, whilst the students largely sit as passive receptors of your pearls of wisdom. At the other end of the scale is the 'discovery' method, where the teacher serves merely as a guide. In general, if you see yourself only in terms of these two extremes, you are probably not doing your job as well as you could. The very best teachers use a wide range of techniques and carefully select the methods and approaches they will use according to what they are trying to teach. So, don't lecture them on learner-centred education!

5 Resources for teaching and learning

You might argue that teachers and learners use different resources in order to fulfil their roles. Somehow, the equipment we tutors use – DVD players, whiteboards and CD-players are our terrain, because the students have learning resources in the shape of books, worksheets, discs and notebooks. I don't see there much of a distinction between them as most of this can be used by students and tutors alike. In some schools, you might be frightened to lend out a pencil. With adults, it is rare to have such problems.

The range of resources is now phenomenal. You are no longer limited to a chalkboard and three pieces of chalk. Most Adult Education Centres and Further Education Colleges have a wide range of equipment available for you to use. In some larger commercial and public organisations they have the very latest gadgetry – often whether they need it or not.

The relentless advance of technology means that there are all sorts of new devices coming onto the market all the time. There is the irresistible rise of DVD, satellite navigation, downloadable TV programming, broadband internet, MP3 (and 4) and mobile phones that are the technological equivalent of the Swiss Army Knife. Soon all these technologies will have converged in such a way and become so cheap, that we'll be stuffing some gadget in our pockets along with a hankie, car keys and some spare change. Yes, the brave new age, when with a click on my handheld device and my teaching notes are shuffled through the either onto your Learnopod™ is probably here already, if not available everywhere. However, it doesn't actually improve the teaching that goes on per se; it just gives skilled tutors more tools that can be used for approaching topics differently. Technology is no substitute for good teaching. Learn some useful methods of showing a film and they apply equally well to a Super8 movie (remember them?) or a DVD. There may be cleverer devices you can now use, but the essentials haven't changed.

Even if your establishment has all the latest gear, you cannot rely on a piece of equipment being available or working or comprehensible to someone without three degrees in electronic engineering. If, like me, you teach in a wide variety of venues a fair distance from home, you are even more at the mercy of forces beyond your control. You arrive to find that your session entitled 'Presentation Skills – Using the Overhead Projector' is in serious jeopardy because there's been a power-cut, which is what happened to me once! As a roving tutor, I'm a great fan of having plenty of material on paper. It's much harder for that to go wrong, although I realise that paper is highly flammable, not particularly robust during the monsoon season and can easily be left on your desk at home. But even bearing in mind these potential disasters, it's still about the safest bet you can make.

If you are going to use some of the larger equipment outlined in these pages, you will need to know the local procedure for booking it. Above all, make sure you are familiar with the equipment you are using. Don't be shy about asking someone for help or a demonstration. You might even find one of your students is an expert and will do it all for you.

Thorough preparation means that you will be able to cope with most disasters, but don't rely on one item of equipment to see you through a session. Carry extras, spares and always have a reserve lesson that doesn't require any gizmos, whatsoever. A good teacher can manage with just a chalk-board (and some chalk).

Audio

Recorded sound is part of this technological revolution. If you are teaching a group of teenagers, most of them will access music via an MP3 player (the iPod being a particular favourite). They will be fully aware of how to download music from the internet and may spend around half their lives with little white ear-pieces jammed down their cochleas, attempting to go deaf.

On the other hand, some have not yet even converted from vinyl or cassette tape. Even if almost everyone nowadays has a CD player, which means that you can make copies of discs for students, some older CD players will not play all the CD formats and you may be breaking copyright, as you can't simply duplicate audio material willy-nilly.

The chances are that your centre's CD player looks like the flight deck of Concorde and has more knobs than the cloakroom at the Ritz. You could spend the first half of the lesson trying to fit the disc into the slot where the batteries should go, so find out how it works beforehand. It may be tempting to bring in your own machine, but you must check local Health and Safety Regulations before so doing.

As with film, it is a little too easy to turn on a CD and expect people simply to listen. Make sure that your students have some positive exercise to do when listening. For language learning, this might be a gap filling exercise, whereby you have transcribed the tape, omitting every tenth word or whatever. For a humanities or social science subject, you could simply ask students to note down the main points of a speaker's argument, before using the resulting answers as a springboard into getting students to give their own opinions.

If you record your own materials, you can give them out as part of an assignment to be done outside class time. Materials recorded from the radio can also be loaned out, but do check about copyright restrictions. With increasing numbers of radio stations offering a 'listen again' facility, you might simply need to point students in the direction of the relevant website.

Chalkboard/whiteboard

Do not sneer at the good old-fashioned chalkboard or its more modern counter-part the whiteboard, which instead of using chalk uses water-soluble, felt-tip pens. No matter what, it remains the greatest piece of equipment in any classroom. If you have not written on a board before, it is worthwhile getting in somewhere and practising, as it is a lot harder than it looks, so here are a few tips:

- If you know what you want to write on the board in a particular session, get into the room beforehand and write it on the board (although it's actually easier to write or print out an OHP acetate or use a computerised slide-show which can then be used again).
- When you have written or drawn something on the board always go to the back of the room to make sure it is clearly visible/legible.
- Don't talk to the board whilst you are writing on it. Your voice will be muffled and it's rude to turn your back on someone when you're speaking to them anyway.
- Don't plant your feet in one place while you are writing. You will find your writing curves away towards the end. Instead of writing in straight lines you will end up with a series of arcs. These will look very pretty, but could seriously damage your students' neck muscles.

Bad board writing is an insult to your students. If you really can't master board work, get hold of an OHP or use PowerPoint instead.

At the end of the session, wipe off what you have written. The next person to use the room doesn't want to have to clean up your mess for you.

Computers and the internet

The personal computer is everywhere nowadays. Even Neanderthal Luddites like me know their way around one, even if we do type with just three fingers. Obviously, there are courses in word-processing, using the internet, or desk-top publishing where using the computer is central to the course. As well as being a vast area of study in their own right, you might like to use a computer, or a suite of computers to teach various topics. For example, students on a Basic English course could produce their own newspaper using a desk-top publishing package. You could use a commercially available educational package, of which there are now hundreds, although most seem to be aimed at the schools market. If you come up with a project or a session that is exciting enough, you often stir up sufficient enthusiasm to overcome all the difficulties.

Some people are scared stiff by computers, hence the proliferation of courses with titles such as 'Computing for the Terrified'. You may find that using a computer merely alienates some of your students, although it can provide a great opportunity for students to learn from each other if you have some students who are computer-literate.

This computer divide can be genuinely problematic. Although there are many older students who can strip a computer down to the hard-drive whilst paragliding blind-folded; others would wonder if the screen was actually just a telly. Similarly, whilst computer prices have tumbled and seem destined to continue to do so, the demands placed on memory, capacity and so forth by increasingly memory-hungry software means that picking up a second-hand device may be inexpensive, but is the equivalent of going on the motorway in a Model-T Ford. The computer is still basically a luxury product and not necessarily the first item on the list for someone earning little.

For retired people, the desk-top computer is essentially a device of the last 15–20 years and if they didn't use them in the workplace, they may not have need for them, although some take up the mouse and keyboard with relish. Given the fact that it's hard enough to programme a DVD recorder, then it's no wonder that many of us stay on the safe soil of old familiar technology for as long as we can.

If you are interested in using computers as an adjunct to your course, it is worth taking some advice, especially if you're not too confident yourself. Computers require a high level of personal skill and knowledge and obviously need a lot of expensive equipment. You may not have used one either at work or in the home. It may be worth taking a computing course yourself – you will not only learn a new skill, but you'll also get the chance to watch another teacher at work.

Computers are our conduit to the internet, which one of the greatest learning resources now available (*the* greatest?). It's a fabulous resource for you as a tutor and a powerful means of enabling your students to become independent learners and researchers. You don't even have to own a computer or have internet access yourself. There are plenty of public libraries with free or cheap access and internet cafés. You will also find that students with an internet facility at home are often extraordinarily generous with their time and skills.

If all your students have access to an internet, it's a great way of keeping them up-to-date. A general email outlining briefly what you did in the class and hand-outs attached means that they feel supported in their work.

At a step further, you may even find yourself teaching via the internet. Internet-based study is a natural progression from the 'correspondence course', where students sent work to tutors for marking and comment. This is dealt with in Chapter 4, should you be reading this book out-of-order!

Flipchart

The flipchart is a free-standing easel-cum-whiteboard to which you can attach a large pad of paper, generally A1 or A2 size (big!). They are very useful for teaching in accommodation where you would not normally find a permanent board, as they are portable. Flipchart paper is also useful for giving out to smaller groups to help them feedback to larger groups. If you're using small group discussion, for instance, feeding back by pinning up their big sheets of paper around the room and talking the rest of the group through points they have made works well.

If you can get hold of a pad of flipchart paper, you can write out beforehand what you would normally write during the session, thereby saving valuable contact time. Another cheeky little method is to write any awkward facts, such as dates or words that are hard to spell, on the pad in very light pencil. When you write in bold on top, citing these facts as if from memory, everyone will think what a wonderful, knowledgeable, intelligent teacher you are.

Just be careful not to mix up your felt-tip pens. You are better off with permanent marker for the paper and non-permanent for the whiteboard. I say this in the full hypocritical knowledge that the other day I wrote on the whiteboard with permanent marker. You'll do it too sometime.

Games

Games can be a useful teaching aid and you don't need to limit them to the last session before Christmas. There are many commercially available games which could be adapted to your needs. You might also like to devise your own in order to teach a certain point. Do try them out first at home, even if you have to imagine that you are all the players. As well as providing a bit of light relief, the game you choose must be relevant to the work you are doing in class. Learners enjoy light-hearted activities, but they are there to learn.

Don't think of 'games' as simply being board games or some equivalent. For example, I often find that in creative writing classes, students are worried that they don't have enough ideas. I take in a little bag full of bits and pieces culled from shelves, drawers or the kitchen. This includes items such as pens, rubber snakes, tiny humour books, old keys, a magnifying glass, bulldog clips, batteries, a packet of mints and mini teddy bears – simply whatever comes to hand. The idea is that each student pulls out an item and has to think of a number of ways in which they could use the object in a story. It's a non-threatening way of getting a lesson rolling, which has the additional intention of showing students that they can take ideas from almost anywhere. In class, they're not put on the spot by having to pluck an idea from thin air and there's an element of luck in what they choose, so there is less of an onus on them to 'be original'.

When using games, everyone needs to be involved. If some people actually don't like the game they can be alienated very quickly. Don't think that anyone who opts out of 'team games' is not being a team player; there may be plenty of other reasons why they don't wish to take part. For instance, commercial training often includes outdoor pursuits games. By learning how to build a suspension bridge over a thousand foot chasm using only seven cornflake boxes and some left-over darning wool, you are suddenly part of a well-oiled human machine that can then solve all the company's problems at a stroke. Of course, it may be a lot of fun (if you like that sort of thing), but the whole concept is flatulent nonsense. If you want to put yourself at the whims and mercy of dangerous psychopaths, then become an international drug smuggler.

Radio and television

In the UK, we are phenomenally lucky to have excellent television and radio programmes. Sure, there's a lot of dross, but there's still some good stuff. Both television and radio are useful sources for teaching materials. The BBC and several of the independent television companies produce programmes specifically for educational purposes. Streaming and downloading programmes (now referred to as podcasting) from the internet will soon become the way in which we all record viewing and listening for later use.

There are also many other programmes that could be used in the classroom. Soap operas often raise important social issues. Documentary and current affairs programmes are useful for a wide variety of subjects. Everyday programmes on cookery, household improvements, history, and the regions – almost anything can be put to some kind of educational use.

Most of the big TV companies also have Education Officers, who might be worth contacting. Record anything that looks useful and read the sections in this chapter on audio and film, for a little homely advice.

Film

At the moment, there are two large shifts taking place with format. The old video-cassette is falling out of use, replaced by DVD, which in turn will soon be replaced or at least added to by hard disk storage. Digital film formats, such as MP4, also means that you can store and play films on tiny hand-held devices, the size of a mobile phone (in fact some are mobile phones).

By the time you read this book, of course, all that may well have changed. However, the essential use of film in a classroom will not. Bluntly, you can either make a film or watch a film (including TV programmes). You are more likely to watch one than make one.

Avoid the trap of thinking that showing a film is a soft option where you can slap in a DVD and have a quick snooze. Most adults attending class in the evening would regard this as something they could easily do at home. And whilst it might be a welcome break for full-time students, it isn't the best use of valuable classroom time. If you are showing a film, make sure that it is relevant, divided into manageable chunks and devise a range of activities to go with it.

It is less likely that you will make films. However, if you do, you could provide students with an exciting and unusual experience. It is not worth making a film for its own sake, but it might be a fun way of examining some of the work they do. For example, if you were teaching a public speaking course or a customer services course, it would provide students with an ideal opportunity for them to examine their techniques, their strengths and where they needed to improve.

If you feel inspired to film activities within your group, have a word with your line manager to find out about availability of equipment. Should it prove impossible to get hold of the necessary equipment within the centre, consider hiring it and splitting the cost among the group.

In the same way as I have suggested that you can email missed handouts to students, it can't be long before the technology to film your lesson and email it to your class is so cheap, that the vast majority of us will be able to do it.

Overhead projector

Normally known as the OHP, this device looks like a square metallic box with a lens on a stalk; which is hardly surprising as this is essentially what it is. In a nutshell, the OHP will take whatever is written on acetate slides (thin sheets of film) and project it onto a flat surface. You may not even have to use a projector screen. You can prepare your own slides, writing directly onto them using either a water or a spirit-soluble pen. If you are making materials you want to keep, it is best to use permanent. If you are computer literate and buy the right kind of acetates for your printer, you can even print them out.

The best thing about the OHP is that you can prepare materials that can be used over and over again with very little loss of quality. The second best thing is that you can mix your permanent and impermanent inks by having a pre-prepared slide to which you can add elements. For example, you could write a gap-filling exercise in which the main part of the sentence is marked permanently and the gap filled in with a water-soluble OHP pen. If you are teaching students how to write a good essay, you could write an example of an essay that needs editing and allow them to edit it on-screen.

It may be a little bit old-fashioned, but I think the OHP is one of the best bits of kit you can have – for almost any subject. Portable ones are even better.

Presentation software

You probably know this by the more common name of PowerPoint, which is the trade name of Microsoft's presentational software. There are equivalents around – indeed within the Open Office suite, which is currently available as a free download from Sun Microsystems, there is an equivalent called simply Presentation. Both programmes are a computerised slide/OHP system that allows you to prepare your work in advance. Of course being able to prepare material in advance is great. The difficulty is that you are left at the multifaceted mercies of computer and software compatibility; the computer has to be linked to a projector; you still need a screen of some description (e.g. projector or TV screen); and it is difficult to change anything you are presenting mid-flow.

There are other pitfalls in using presentation software. It goes by that name for a reason. It is really designed for helping to illustrate a lecture and, whilst being able to give students printed copies of what is on your slide show is very useful, it doesn't stop what you're doing from merely being a pimped-up lecture.

PowerPoint tends to find its natural home in those awful corporate 'ra-ra' sessions. Is it any wonder that the phrase 'Death by PowerPoint' has entered the language? The phrase may be a little harsh on the creators of what is a clever piece of software. I reserve my most vitriolic spleen for the 'presenters' who think that by including little animations and gizmos are actually making their talk more interesting. They are actually detracting from the job and are as likely to be covering up for the lack of meat in the sandwich by using posh bread.

Slides

Most centres or colleges used to have a slide projector hidden in a cupboard somewhere. Very few have a slide library. If you are going to show slides, the likelihood is that you will have to provide or even produce your own. Slides are a very useful way of sharing pictures with the whole group. Using slides in a lecture is a good method of ensuring that it is not simply you talking all the time; on the other hand, the pitfall is that what was intended to be a slide-show could simply become an illustrated lecture.

Encourage comments from your students. Ask them to bring along their own relevant slides or pictures. Keep it lively. If your topic is Greek Architecture and you have taken the slides yourself while on a family holiday, avoid showing the one of Auntie Lil in front of the Acropolis, unless it is to show the scale of the building.

Again, computers linked to a monitor or TV screen are taking over from slides, but the essence remains the same.

Making your own materials

Pop into any decent bookshop (if such a beast still exists) and you will see loads of ready-made materials for teaching most subjects. However, many of these are geared towards subjects that carry some kind of certification. It isn't always possible to find appropriate material for your subject if the course is of your own devising. Even if you are teaching something for which there is a useful course book, you will find that your lessons go so much better if you create your own resources. If you do this, you will soon build up a range of appropriate, tailored materials that you can use again and again.

A teacher of glass painting might like to create a whole series of examples to show students that will help them to see what possibilities exist. A woodwork tutor might like to create a range of joints as examples for the students. A modern languages tutor might collect everyday items. Packaging materials brought back from abroad can add realism to a lesson on shopping. Tutors of Basic Skills can use an old kitchen clock to help practise telling the time.

There is no doubt that creating your own teaching aids is a very positive thing to do. It can also be very time-consuming. The time you invest in creating your own materials must pay off in your classes. To spend four hours preparing for an activity that will last five minutes in class is very noble, but probably a waste of effort. Don't reinvent the wheel. If you've seen something used successfully before, adapt it for your own teaching.

Tutor's portfolio

It might be worth building up a portfolio of examples of your own work that students can look through for ideas. For some subjects, this might just be a file or folder; for others you might have to put together a box of examples. For instance, if you are teaching paper-making, you could carry with you a series of samples to show students what they can achieve. A little time spent tying a few knots and mounting them on a board will show students learning to sail what their end products should look like. Some photographs of the various stages of the construction of a larger item can also help students see the way in which they are going. Portfolios such as these take ages to do. However, if you are planning to teach your subject for some time, they can be worthwhile. They also have the added side-effect of making you think through the entire process as a learner, rather than a tutor.

Handouts

It is often worth preparing handouts for your group. Handouts could perform a number of different functions, e.g. act as ready-made lecture notes, summarise a particular topic or act as an introduction to the next topic. Handouts can also come in the form of worksheets, which are a good way of moving away from the rigid course-book approach. Adult students seem to love getting handouts, although I recently had feedback from a student on the huge number of handouts. 'What about all those trees?' she said. She's right, but it's the old ingrained habit of working in borrowed accommodation. You can't carry loads of equipment, so you make sure you've got plenty of handouts. A lot of teachers call them 'happy sheets'. If people go away from a course with lots of bits of paper that they can peruse at their leisure, then they are contented. This is a little bit cynical, but there is an enormous core of truth in it. Handouts are one of the most useful learning aids that you can supply. Good teachers make a huge variety of them with very different aims in mind.

Handouts for reference

These are great for students to put in their files or folders. Book lists, contact lists, jargon-busters for your subject, vocabulary lists for language learning, diagrams and so forth all make useful reference handouts, for use at home and in your classes. A well-designed handout is useful for a practical subject, even if you don't actually use it in the session. These are not quite teaching aids in themselves, but should provide students with additional information.

Students often see these as a bit of a bonus. It cuts down on their personal research time and points them in the right direction. It can also help their confidence incredibly, if they do not keep on having to ask you to clarify a point over and over again, simply because they've forgotten.

Note-taking handouts

As mentioned earlier, a handout with a few bullet-points can be very useful to guide students' note-taking. For example, you can use an overhead projector or a whiteboard to put up your main points. The students can write their own notes around your bullet points. This can also be used to make a PowerPoint-style presentation more interesting. The difficultly is knowing if you should provide all your 'slides' in advance or not. If you do, then students may well read ahead and miss the points you are making. If you hand out copies slide-by-slide, then it can be very time-consuming.

Worksheets

These will vary enormously according to your subject and the level of the group. The simplest worksheets might include word searches or pictures that need naming. More advanced examples may ask students to give highly complex replies. Worksheets are an excellent way of helping you to focus your teaching on a particular point. For instance, in a mathematics class, you can explain on the board how to calculate the hypotenuse. Then, with a worksheet, you can give a further example and ask students to work through a dozen or so examples. Whilst they're doing this, it gives you a chance to scoot round the class ensuring that your students have grasped the idea. Making your worksheets means you can control the 'portion'. Students are not overwhelmed by hundreds of pages of textbook.

Don't forget that it is very easy to lose a worksheet or handout. We all know how we can search our houses from attic to cellar for a particular item, only to find it two years later when eventually we move the fridge to clean behind it. Always keep a few spare copies. Students who've missed a class or forgotten or lost their sheets will really appreciate the way you can solve what they will perceive as a problem. Also, remember the tip about emailing missed sheets.

When using a worksheet for the first time, keep a copy on one side and, if anything does not work particularly well, mark up the copy and change it the next time you use it.

Worksheets and handouts should:

- be attractive to the learner – we don't want to put them off with a poor design
- have plenty of 'white space' – gaps between paragraphs, good margins
- be written in a good-sized font – at the very least 10, but preferably 12 or even 14 point
- have relevant pictures and diagrams
- use headings, sub-headings and bullet points
- leave room to complete exercises (you need twice as much space to handwrite as you do to type)

- be straightforward – you're trying to teach, not baffle
- be checked for spelling, grammar and punctuation mistakes (so it's best to prepare them ages in advance and then proofread them later).

Dictation

Dictation has gone completely out of fashion. I suspect that it is because a generation of teachers bored their students rigid by 'dictating notes', a favourite technique amongst O-Level teachers of yore.

I suspect that dictating notes is one of the greatest wastes of a student's time known unto civilisation. However, there are other forms of dictation that can be useful for certain types of class. English and Modern Language classes can both benefit from occasional spurts of dictation. It genuinely helps with spelling. However, it is best to keep dictation short and, rather than 'mark' it, give the passage or series of words to the students for them to check themselves. Try not to include any words that they are unlikely to have come across. Don't forget that if you put the correct version on an OHP or board, those people with reading difficulties might find it hard to retain the image of the words between looking up at your version and down at their own.

It's best not to swap papers for marking, as that can put students on the spot. Students will often compare notes of their own accord and it can be a powerful way of enabling them to learn from one another. I would still use it sparingly.

Comprehension

We all remember comprehensions from our schooldays. Frequently, it was a case of reading through a passage, culled from some obscure nineteenth-century historian, after which we were then expected to answer questions that varied from the inane to the obscure.

Comprehension is an excellent aid to learning, especially in the humanities, Social Sciences and Languages. The real trick is to make a comprehension relevant to your students.

Giving instructions

There's an old adage amongst teachers – 'Tell them what you're going to tell them, tell them, then tell them what you've told them.' It may sound cynical, but it's quite useful technique that's also often used in textbooks and academic books. The introduction to a chapter or unit 'Tells them what you're going to tell them'. The main body of the unit 'tells them', and then the conclusion 'tells them what you've told them'.

Imagine you are about to get students to use a piece of gym equipment – a rowing machine, for example. You might explain the parts of the machine, then get on the machine and show them how it's done and then get a volunteer to climb onto the machine and guide them through it.

This is, of course, partly a demonstration, but you are also giving instructions on how to use the rowing machine. By breaking it down into three steps – your explanation, your demonstration and guiding a student through using the machine as an example, you have 'told them what you're going to tell them, told them and told them what you've told them'. As have I in this little section, thereby making me feel extremely smug.

It is worth thinking about the instructions you give in order to make them as clear as possible. As a student, there can be nothing more embarrassing than having misunderstood what the tutor said, to find that you're the only one out of step.

Assignments

A lot of tutors tend to use the word 'assignment' to mean 'homework'. Fearing that the word homework smacks too much of schooldays, they think 'assignment' sounds better. They may have a point. On the other hand, 'assignments' are what James Bond would go on. It's pretty difficult imagining some cross-stitch practice or 'taking a few photos of anything red' as being on a par with paragliding away from the evil forces of SMERSH.

You will have to negotiate assignments with your group. In weekly adult education classes, it can be quite difficult to expect students to produce regular weekly work. I think this also depends on the course. Students on a course that leads to certification will almost certainly have to do work outside the class.

For 'leisure'-oriented classes, the idea of voluntary homework is a good one. Try to make the homework something that will stretch the students into some additional skill or practise one they have just learnt, rather than making it the basis of your next teaching session. Anyone who has not done the work, for whatever reason, may feel left out. They may even drop out of your class because they don't want to be shown up. Stating how much additional work you expect students to do is helpful. Often students are keen to have a course whereby what they do doesn't just stop when the caretaker locks up for the evening.

You must be realistic, though. Whilst an hour's contact time in a University probably needs matching by ten hours' study from a full-time student, you can't expect your weekly leisure painters to put in twenty hours away from the class.

I once read an opinion column in an art magazine, where an artist who also worked as an adult education tutor upbraided her students for not doing enough work. It ran along the lines of 'I went to art college for seven years and devote at least 40 hours a week to painting, so how can students who only pick up a paint brush in my class expect to be as good as Monet...' I can see how it might be annoying that your students don't put in a 40 hour week on your subject, but you have to accept that they are human and have commitments elsewhere. If hoping to be Monet in a week is an unreasonable expectation, say so at the start of the class. Most students appreciate honesty.

When you are setting assignments, allow individuals to choose their own work whenever you think it is practical or possible. For instance, if you are teaching a craft-based subject and someone is engaged on a project, they may simply need some advice on which aspect of the work to tackle next. Others might want more leading. There is, of course, little reason why everyone in a class has to be doing the same thing all the time.

Books

As colleges, schools and universities transform their libraries into 'resource centres', so the good old fashioned book loses its footing as the most important element of education. You can moan about this as much as you want, but you can't hold back the forces of technology.

Books, however, are still a vital part of the educational process. Most important for trainers and tutors is the course book, but don't forget the importance of the general reading book. Sometimes they will be one and the same thing. For instance, the book you are now reading aims to be a general reader on adult education, but could equally well be read as a starting-point for a course on training the trainer or teaching adults.

A number of subjects in mainstream adult education are badly served by course books. They are or may be aimed at younger people, be too theoretical, or too simplistic – which brings us back to making our own materials.

Work-related subjects tend to be better catered for. There are innumerable books on time management, management techniques, selling, running a small business, work-based assessment and so on. For most adult students, books on the subject are more of a way of 'reading round' what they are doing. Producing a useful booklist and/or list of internet sites will help those who want to read and research further. You may also find that your students, once they start helping one another, will bring in books of their own to lend to other people. Students on a course on interior design for the home, for instance, might bring in books to give you some idea of the look they are trying to achieve in their bathroom or to discuss with other students what elements of a particular design they might go for.

The great thing about books is that anyone can join their local public library, which usually means that they can borrow books for free. You may find that your students are actually a little wary of joining a library. They may not think of it as the kind of place for them. In this case, they need some gentle encouragement.

The free public library system is one of the gems of civilisation.

And finally...when designing tasks

When designing any kind of task – handout, case study, practical work, or whatever – you need to think through the various stages a student will have to follow. Most tasks are successful if you use the following criteria:

- There is an obvious step-by-step progression through the task.
- The task is meaningful – it has some kind of learning outcome.
- Where possible it is related to real life.
- The task is interesting.

- The different elements of the task involve different kinds of exercises.
- Students can tell if they have completed the task successfully.
- It must be of the correct level for students or have different levels of achievement within it.

Then, when you've prepared all these materials, you can plug the gap in the textbook market by putting them together in book form.

6   Assessment and evaluation

If you're new to the terms 'assessment' and 'evaluation', you may well think that they seem interchangeable. In most situations they are, but in education, they are not. Assessment is all about checking your students' progress and achievements; evaluation is to do with making judgements about how well your course, your lessons and your teaching are going.

Assessment

Assessing your students is an integral part of any course. Obviously as more and more courses carry formal qualifications, then assessment is an integral part. Often you'll find the language used to describe the assessments off-putting. If that is the case, then simply get hold of an example of the assessment. What does it actually look like? Traditionally, we had exams and essays and projects. Nowadays there is a whole range of ways in which students are assessed. For instance, many courses are validated by the Open College Network. It is possible to have them accredit a course you are running. The types of assessment they are looking for are contained in the fabric of the course itself. If you were teaching an embroidery class, it's quite reasonable that students will produce a piece of embroidery. This work is both intrinsic to the course and also accreditable under certain schemes.

This leads us naturally to realise that assessing your students does not merely apply to those courses that have formalised systems of certification. Assessment is vital for both you and your students to make judgements about their progress. If you have external validation of what you are doing, students have some kind of standard against which to measure themselves – it is actually harder where there is no external yardstick. To an extent, that means that the assessment of students in non-accredited courses is even more important.

Student assessment begins at the very first session. As adults are this funny mix of different experiences, skills and knowledge, one of the first things you are going to have to do is assess what your students already know or can do. This can be very hard. One way to assess your students is to give them a little entry 'test'. You can get away with this if you make the test fairly broad and non-threatening. However, it's always worth putting yourself in the place of your students. How might you feel if you wandered along to a flower arranging class and found that before you were allowed to start you had to make a Christmas wreath just to see how good you were?

On the other hand, if you're going to take a higher level qualification, then knowing that you are capable of working at that level is useful. You might even welcome an entry test before shelling out the increasingly large fees demanded.

In a mainstream adult education class, you can assess your new students fairly informally, although increasingly colleges are handing out generic forms – often completely irrelevant to your subject – so that somewhere, someone can fiddle with statistics to prove something we either knew already or didn't need to know anyway. If you can adapt these forms, do. The real problem is that students, already hacked off with questions that many feel intrusive (race, disability, etc.) just can't stand the sight of yet another form. My tip is to sell these forms to students on the basis that the course is subsidised and that filling it in is saving them money. It doesn't always work. 'I think I'd rather just pay,' comes back the quip.

You can also make good initial judgments quite informally. Create a supportive atmosphere by your kindness, empathy and humour and you will soon have people telling you of their prior experiences. If you don't feel confident doing that, then wheedle out some relevant information over coffee, which is probably the best time to slap the forms in front of them anyway. One great tip I picked up was that if you do your own form to find out about prior knowledge (something gentle, rather than a 'test'), write somewhere near the top 'To help me with my teaching and to prepare our lessons, I'd be extremely grateful if...'. Students will do things for their friendly tutor that they won't do for the pen-pushing children of Kafka.

Obviously, asking a handful of questions is not a very scientific approach, but it is better than having no prior assessment at all. At the other end of the scale comes what is normally referred to as APL or APEL, which stands for Accreditation of Prior Learning (or Experience and Learning). The idea behind this is that students can be given credit for things that they have already learnt or accomplished informally, or at work, before they have joined your course. This is often a dull tick-box exercise, but at least it can prove to the learner that they are not the complete beginner that they feared.

Formative, summative and continuous assessment

Once you have ascertained prior levels of skills, knowledge and experience, you will want to assess progress and achievement.

Formative assessment is the kind of assessment that you will do as the course progresses. For instance, in Maths, you need to be able to multiply before you can move on to the concept of squares. Formative assessment would help you to check this. Once you have covered the topic of multiplication, you will want to test your students' ability to use it. You might choose to ask a few questions around the class, or the accrediting body of the course that you are teaching might call for some kind of interim test as part of continuous assessment. Whatever method you use, you are still assessing as you go along to ensure that learning has taken place. Once you are convinced your students can multiply, you can then move on to teaching them squares.

Formative assessment is not just for your students. It is also vital for you as a tutor. If you find that your students have not learnt something particularly well, you may well decide that you need to revise that particular area of weakness. This is also sometimes known as diagnostic testing. It also allows you to adjust your course plan (or programme of study or planned learning sequence or whatever the latest appalling jargon might be) according to what your students need to know.

Summative assessment, on the other hand, takes place at the end of a unit or a course. It is a method of assessing what learning has taken place during the course. Traditionally, summative assessment has taken the form of examinations. These may not be entirely relevant for your students. However, they need some form of assessment; otherwise they may not think that they have made any progress. It doesn't have to be too formal – a quiz, a competition, comparing recent work with earlier efforts – an activity that tests progress without screaming 'I am testing your progress'. Summative assessment is vital. It tells you whether or not your students have had their money's worth.

You may also come across the term 'continuous assessment'. This is like a combination of summative and formative assessment. Instead of saving everything up for one big final test, students are assessed at various stages of the course. It is increasingly popular throughout the education system. There are advantages to it. No longer are you reliant on not having hay-fever on the day of your exam, hoping the right question comes up or keeping yourself awake with overdoses of caffeine. On the other hand, the series of lower hurdles that students are expected to jump on a more frequent basis, can lower standards. Learning tends to be compartmentalised. There is less steady accretion of knowledge, skills and abilities.

Mostly adult students like continuity of assessment. It enables them to set a series of shorter-term goals. Success in the first assessment will give them a positive outlook for the next step. Also, quite frankly, how would you like to spend three hours in an examination hall nowadays without coffee, a packet of rich tea biscuits and easy access to the toilet?

It's not all rosy for students though. Continuous assessment often carries with it a large workload, which can occasionally be daunting, especially to students whose previous experiences of education have not been entirely positive.

Some assessment strategies

If you are teaching an informal, non-exam class, such as Tai Chi or Music Appreciation, you will probably want to teach in an informal style. It would come as an enormous shock to students if, having been laid back with them all year, chatting over coffee and creating an air of relaxed purpose; you suddenly whip out a formal examination paper on the last day.

For informal courses, the best form of assessment is also informal. Students may be aware that they are being assessed by you, but they won't think of it as a 'test'. They will soon realise that you are assessing them so that you know more about them and their progress. Most students will thoroughly appreciate this.

Knowing your students individually, appreciating the way they work, understanding what makes them tick all goes into the mix that enables you to make judgments about their progress.

At the end of each session, it is worth spending a few minutes checking to see if the students have grasped what you have done. There are many different ways in which you can do this. If you're teaching a craft subject, you can do this almost surreptitiously. If your topic for this evening's electrical class was wiring a lighting circuit, then you can simply spend the last ten minutes seeing if the circuits actually work. You could check on a knowledge-based course by having a little quiz.

If you prefer something a little more upfront, you could restate the aims and learning outcomes for the particular session and ask students if they feel they have achieved this. But the danger with harking on too much about the learning outcomes is that students often 'just want to get on with it'. They can see this as taking up their precious learning time with unnecessary silliness and waffle.

I suspect it is probably best to leave formal assessment out of the adult education classroom unless you are teaching the kind of course that means it is unavoidable. These will largely be accredited courses. Be warned, however, nowadays, the accent is definitely on accreditation. Even courses that are being pursued for the sheer enjoyment of learning may carry some kind of qualification if they are to have any form of public funding. If this is the case with the course you are teaching, it is well worth investigating what alternatives there are to 'proper' exams. Organisations such as the aforementioned Open College Network are keen to give credit to adult students for what they have achieved without making the assessment process too obvious.

Self and peer assessment

Learning how to assess your own progress is an extremely useful skill for the learner. You may find that a lot of students who drop out of a course do so because they 'don't feel they're making progress'. They may actually be making terrific progress, but they have nothing against which to measure it.

When students assess how much progress they have made, they generally underestimate themselves. If they have just undergone some form of assessment and had feedback from it, they will be better placed to make these judgements.

When you can already do something at a high level, it is often very difficult indeed to work out what progress you are making. It becomes harder to quantify. As a beginner, checking progress is often straight-forward. In a swimming class for beginners, for example, you might first learn to float, and then swim a width, then a length, then two. Progress is obvious and measurable. Deepening one's understanding of Shakespeare, on the other hand, is something far harder to measure. Helping students to assess themselves by giving them assessment tasks they can carry out themselves is an excellent way of doing this. You can quite easily convert the language of your learning outcomes into more straight-forward English and create a tick sheet relevant to your subject.

For an introductory course on teaching adults, such a list might contain the following sorts of statements:

I can:

Identify five common barriers to learning	Confidently	Need practice
Explain the term 'learning outcome'	Confidently	Need practice
Design a worksheet for use in the classroom	Confidently	Need practice
Write legibly on the board	Confidently	Need practice
Operate the centre's DVD player	Confidently	Need practice
Design an OHP transparency	Confidently	Need practice
Create an assessment exercise	Confidently	Need practice

Of course, these would be better divided into more logical sections, but I'm sure you get the idea.

If you want your learners to develop autonomy, self-assessment is a great way to get them doing it. Peer assessment is another method. This has the advantage of helping the group to gel if it is done well. You may often find that whilst individual students underestimate their achievements, others in the class are quick to show them just how much they are learning.

There's nothing like a bit of approval and applause from your classmates to bolster you up. If you can encourage your students to give one another feedback in a positive way, then it helps the group and the individuals.

Remember

Whatever form of assessment you use, you should feed the results back to your students as soon as possible. Sometimes, there are checks and balances in place on your assessment. Someone else may need to sample your marking to make sure that it is of the right standard. If that's the case, tell the students this. Otherwise, it may seem to them that their hard work has simply vanished into the dark hole of 'the system'.

You need to take a positive approach to giving back work. Some people may be sorely disappointed with their results. You need to help those students who are dissatisfied with their marks, give appropriate praise and look for constructive ways of moving your students on to the next stage of their learning. If you negotiate learning targets with your students, so that they have a personal investment in what they are going to learn, you will find that they are much more willing to be assessed. This includes explaining to the students, collectively and individually, what they could do next time that would improve their work.

Make any assessment as relevant as you can to your subject. If you have been teaching Yoga, check to see that your students are capable of demonstrating the postures you have taught. If you are teaching flower arranging, get them to do a special seasonal display (for Christmas for instance), in which they can show off the various techniques they've learnt. If they have been studying antiques, do a little 'Going for a Song' session in which the students are given an antique to identify. If your students are studying website design, get them to make a website for themselves, their businesses or as a hobbyist site. There is no need for assessment to be turgid. In fact, if you're really good, you can turn it into something of a lark.

So, to sum up, effective assessment:

- is relevant to the subject
- is applied in a practical situation
- is as unobtrusive as it can be
- is directly related to learning outcomes and aims
- allows the tutor to revise the course or session plan as appropriate
- gives students a sense of achievement
- motivates the learner to carry on
- helps learners identify what they need to do next
- enables the tutor to check existing knowledge or skills before moving on to the next stage
- works even better if it involves the student and the group directly.

Learners need positive, constructive feedback from themselves, their peers and you, the tutor. They need to be given it clearly, in a supportive atmosphere and as soon as possible. Assessment isn't just a case of throwing your students on the mercy of an accrediting body; it's about helping them make progress and be aware of how much progress they are making.

Evaluation

Evaluation, I'm afraid, is much harder than assessment. With evaluation, you are either having to make judgements about your own work as a tutor (perhaps based on student feedback), or getting someone in to watch you teach. It's very hard for us to make judgements about ourselves and our work. Just like our own students, we often become either much too harsh about our own performance or far too uncritical. It's also easy to identify when something is good or bad, but harder to state clearly what needs improvement.

As someone who is going to evaluate your own teaching, you need to be critical of your course, the sessions you teach and your performance as a teacher. Being critical does not mean that you have to judge yourself severely and merely look for weaknesses. It's also about identifying strengths, deciding what activities work, what don't, what seems to motivate your group, how you relate to students, how you manage your class and the whole range of activities that make up this process of teaching.

To evaluate your own performance, you have to imagine that you are observing someone else teach. Yes, you want to point out things that could have been done better, but you also want to praise them for the good work they have done. You can be truthful without being vicious. Being self-critical does not mean being nasty to yourself. That way madness lies.

Similarly, don't think of evaluation as a luxury add-on extra. It is an important part of teaching, which starts right at the beginning of the teaching process. Think constantly about your teaching style, methods, materials and all the component elements of your teaching.

You do not have to attempt to evaluate on your own. You must involve your students by encouraging them to feed in their own ideas – not just at one formal point, but throughout the teaching and learning process. This can be done fairly simply. Informal chats over coffee work well (you can see that the coffee break is a bit of a theme in this book!). You can even ask students directly. 'I've never tried doing this exercise before, so I'd be pleased if you could let me know if you think it works.' If you create a rapport with your students, you will soon find that you get feedback automatically without asking for it.

Not everyone will like every exercise you do. We know that people learn in very different ways. However, a class taking its lead from the tutor, where the students develop mutual trust and respect will generally be adaptable. Yet again, we come down to the fact that you, as the tutor, must set the lead in terms of the general attitude that the students will have towards you and others. This is fine for day-to-day evaluation, but sometimes you do need something a little more formal.

Formal evaluation

Most educational establishments ask for some kind of feedback from their students at the end of a course. This is fine, for a one-day or short course, but is less effective on longer courses. If it is distributed after ten, fifteen, maybe thirty weeks, the students who have the most adverse comments to make have probably long since given up the course, so you may only get feedback off the ones who are largely happy. The kinds of evaluation sheets used for this purpose are often general, produced in-house, to cover every subject from basic manicure tech-niques to degrees in Psychology. You want to know if your session on how plants cross-pollinate made sense; the centre's form has a vague question about satisfac-tion with the general standard of teaching.

Some institutions whip the evaluation forms off you as soon as the students fill them in. You get a couple of minutes to glance at them before they disappear into the bowels of the organisation to be number-crunched into a spreadsheet. This is not particularly useful for you as a tutor. You should ask to see the evaluation forms or, if possible, make copies for yourself. It is only by being able to evalu-ate your work that you can make improvements, adjustments and alterations to what you do. We all want to be better teachers.

But don't dismiss this kind of general evaluation form entirely. If the institution or department can turn round and tell the people with the purse strings that 95 per cent of students found the standard of teaching good or very good, it probably won't harm their funding prospects. Nor should you dismiss it on a personal level. Your students telling the powers-that-be that they found your teaching good is a genuine pat on the back. We all need praise from time to time. No, don't dismiss it, but take it with a pinch of salt. You need proper feedback, but you need it in a way that will be useful to you.

It is worthwhile constructing some form of evaluation sheet which can be used at the end of a term or after a topic. The questions you ask will depend on your subject. If you teach Art, you might like to know if there is any demand for a session on History of Art. If you teach Languages, it is useful to know if you are getting the grammar/conversation mix right. If you teach Physical Exercise, you might like to know if the activities feel too strenuous or not.

If you do decide to create your own form, it is important to make sure that the questions are straightforward to answer. It is not an exercise in scientific discovery, so you can make it quite chatty. If you've done scholarly research, there's no need to worry about how scientific this approach is.

What should you ask?

To an extent, what you ask is up to you. All teachers have their personal preferences. There are many different ways you can ask for feedback. All of them have their advantages and their disadvantages. Don't think that you have to find one way of doing it and stick to that. Experiment until you find a way that suits your subject.

General comments

You can simply hand round a piece of paper and ask students to write down what they feel about the course. If you want, you can narrow this down by asking for three comments about a particular session. This method does allow students to say what they want. However, it may be harder for students with limited literacy skills and it is possible for students to omit something, because there is nothing on the sheet to remind them.

Number-crunching

You can ask questions in this kind of format:

Was the pre-course information useful?	1	2	3	4	5
Were the handouts useful?	1	2	3	4	5
What was the standard of teaching?	1	2	3	4	5

(1=poor, 5=excellent)

This is the kind of method that institutions use, because they can more quickly and easily get the results together for analytical purposes.

Some people don't like numbers – they find them off-putting. You may find people who have misread the numbering system and given you a grade 1 for everything, indicating that your teaching is dire, when they've patently enjoyed the course tremendously, and were forever telling you how good a teacher you are. You can do the same sort of thing by asking people to ring a word or a little phrase, e.g.

How much progress do you think you have made?

A lot   Quite a lot   Some   Not a lot   None at all

It's just a variation. You can still give the responses a numerical value for analytical purposes, and it is perhaps easier for us to give praise to tutors in this way – and we need praise as well as criticism. I'm sure that many of us find it hard to give 5 out of 5 – 'you can't get full marks, it's impossible!' – but are prepared to say that something is excellent.

Broader feedback

Treading carefully between the heavily guided approach and simply asking for general comments, you can easily compromise on the kind of evaluation form that asks for comments, but in a guided format.

If you make up such a form, you will obviously want to tailor it to your subject. However, there are certain aspects that any evaluation form should cover:

- enjoyment
- teaching
- level of course
- handouts/worksheets
- assignments
- exercises
- equipment used
- progress
- anything need revising
- additional comments.

Caveat 1 – Form-filling fatigue

The 'customer as king' is now so ingrained in most aspects of our culture that customers are forever being asked to fill in feedback forms. Go down to your local branch of a burger bar and there's probably a questionnaire for you to fill in about cleanliness, quality of service, freshness of food and so forth. It takes longer to fill in than it does to eat the burger and will certainly pass through the system more slowly. You can inundate people with the need for some kind of feedback. You should, therefore, make your form easy to complete and, if your institution has its own form, try not to give them out at the same time (if indeed you do two at all).

Caveat 2 – Who said that?

Anonymity can also be an issue. Whenever I go on a course and am given an evaluation form, I always put my name on the form, whether it is asked for or not.

This is because I think that if I am going to say something to a tutor, they have a right to know that it is me who has said it.

I know other people who feel that if they are not asked for their name, they can be more truthful. I've spoken to several experienced tutors on this issue and the general consensus is that it is best not to ask for names, but to suggest that students can write their names on the form if they so wish.

Caveat 3 – Contradictory feedback

'We concentrated too much on marketing,' writes one student on your Starting a Small Business course. 'I don't think we covered marketing well enough,' writes another. Bluntly, you can't win them all. Several tutors I spoke to said that they felt that these kinds of criticisms cancelled one another out and became 'neutral'. I think that's fair enough.

Caveat 4 – Odd feedback

Occasionally, you will get bizarre feedback that you can't fathom. I once taught a public one-day course and was thrilled with the positive comments on the first few forms. People had paid for this course out of their own pockets and had obviously got their money's worth. I was chuffed at a job so expertly well done. No one in the entire history of adult education had got such positive feedback. It was only a short while before the District Council would be round to stick a circular blue plaque on the front of my house. The whole area would take pride in the fact that such a brilliant adult educator should choose to grace the town with his presence.

Pride cometh before a fall. Whilst I was busy preening myself, I turned to the next form which said 'A much more pleasant experience than I anticipated'. What? I re-read it. Did they mean that it was a pleasant experience or that; despite the fact it was me teaching it, it wasn't too bad? Or what? I still don't know to this day whether that was a positive or a negative comment. It sticks in the mind, though.

Another good one I once had was 'Management is purely a tool for the oppression of workers'. It sounds more like an item of graffiti from Paris in May 1968 than a comment on a course – especially as I wasn't even part of the management.

Other forms of student feedback – attendance

Very few Adult Education courses still boast the same number of students at the end of the course as they did at the beginning. Your register will provide you with some kind of guide for this.

However, it is very important that you try to retain your students. The level of attendance at your course and the level of dropout are two ways in which you can judge for yourself how successful the course has been. They are *not* the only ways.

Students drop out of courses for a whole variety of reasons. Some fall ill, move house, change their shifts, can no longer afford it... or a whole host of reasons which are beyond your control. Others drop out because they are dissatisfied with the teaching, their fellow students, they lack confidence... they've missed two weeks because they were on holiday and don't think they can catch up. These are factors over which you can have some control.

If someone has missed two sessions without giving a reason, contact them and try to find out why they have been absent. It might simply be that they forgot to tell you about a holiday commitment. It might be that they are in some way unhappy about the class. Discuss with them the problem. The very fact that you are open to discussion will help them to return to your class.

Other forms of student feedback – observation as evaluation

You should consider getting someone to visit your class to observe you at work. It is best if this person is a professional adult educator who understands enough about your subject to make useful comments. Make sure that you provide any observer with a copy of your course and session plan, as well as handouts, books or other materials.

If you are being observed on a peer review basis, rather than as part of some kind of inspection or appraisal process, decide beforehand what your observer should be looking for and commenting on. I would suggest that you could do worse than start with a list like this:

- your overall course preparation
- how well you have prepared this particular session
- the room layout
- your use of teaching equipment
- the variety of the methods you use
- your subject knowledge
- how you communicate with your students
- the appropriateness of the learning resources you have chosen
- how well you have designed any of your own teaching resources (e.g. handouts)
- your relationship with the students
- the students' involvement in the session
- the techniques you use to assess student progress.

If you can't find a professional to observe you teach, then get someone who has tons of common sense and good judgement and who will be kind (but not uncritical) about your work. Rather than have them observe from some corner of the room, you might invite them to join in as a student. You can then ask them to comment on more general issues concerning the way in which you deal with students.

A list for this kind of evaluation might include such ideas as observing if you:

- seem flexible
- show tact and diplomacy

- encourage your students
- make the learning interesting
- are approachable
- seem interested in your students
- are enthusiastic
- seem confident
- deal with any difficult situations well.

Frankly, by inviting people into your classroom, you will be learning an enormous amount. It also shows that you are confident enough in your teaching to have someone else come in and feedback to you afterwards.

These days, with greater accountability, you are much more likely to be observed formally in the classroom. You will find that by having visitors from time-to-time, you soon get used to the idea that your classroom is not closed to others. When you do have some kind of formal observation or inspection, you will feel less apprehensive about it and might even welcome it. If you are observed in this formal way, find out from the observer what their experience of adult education is, if they still teach adults on a regular basis and, if not, when they last did so. The opinion of someone who is still actively teaching – even if not as often as they once did – is worth far more than that of any desk-jockey.

Conclusion

Evaluation and assessment are not the same thing. You assess your students' progress and you evaluate the success of your teaching. You must carry out both throughout your classes and at the end of a term, a topic, or a block of learning.

Try to match assessment and evaluation to your course. By ensuring that students have discernible and achievable targets for their learning, it is both easier to assess them and to evaluate your course.

Wherever possible, try not to be too formal in either. Testing students all the time does not mean that they are necessarily learning anything extra. Just think of all the stuff you crammed into your skull during your own schooldays for a test the next day that you couldn't recall now if it would save you from a firing squad. Above all, make it obvious to your students that you are there to help them, that you appreciate their comments and feedback and that you are in partnership together to help them with their learning. If they know that their progress and learning matter to you, then you are half-way there.

7 Planning

Planning a course

Before you get into the classroom and start teaching, you will need to plan your course. If you are studying on a teacher training course, 'course planning', which seems a perfectly good way of describing exactly what you're going to do, may be described by any one of a number of ugly terms: 'Planning a sequence of learning' is one that gets bandied about a great deal. I've even heard 'Designing sequential learning experiences'.

It's all course planning. Just because some people give it a silly name, doesn't make it a silly process; course planning is vital. After all, you need to know what you're doing and your students will appreciate knowing where they're going.

With general adult education courses, you may have the luxury of being able to devise your own course. On the other hand, you might be given an 'off-the-peg' course to teach. Accreditation bodies will have syllabuses for their qualifications, but you will still have to turn a syllabus into a coherent teaching plan.

No matter what kind of course you are teaching, you must plan. If there is an existing syllabus for a course, you may find it written in a style that is very off-putting. There is a tendency in education at the moment to write everything in the most hideous, mangled English. National Vocational Qualifications are especially bad for this. If you're having difficulty understanding the syllabus, just think how hard it might be for your students!

This chapter deals with planning a course of your own devising from scratch. Most of what I have to say applies equally to courses based on existing syllabuses (they're often called schemes nowadays).

If you are able to devise your own course from scratch, you may have plenty of leeway. Some people like the freedom to be able to devise their own courses. Don't expect to be able to plan everything at once. It is worth spending as much time over it as possible. Keep a notebook especially devoted to your course planning and add to your ideas over time. At some point you will feel as though you have the makings of a course and will then be able to start consolidating these notes into a coherent plan.

When your course plan is complete, it should contain the following:

- course title
- your target students, including the level of the course

- length and timing of the course, e.g. 20 weeks at 3 hours per week
- aim(s) of the course
- learning outcomes
- topics
- general statement of methods
- teaching and learning resources needed (no need to be too specific at this stage – a general statement will do).

There are other things that you could include, but most of them are best left to the session planning stage, when you are getting down to the nitty-gritty of deciding exactly how you are going to teach the various elements of your course plan.

What is the title of your course?

You don't have to think of a name for your course immediately, but it helps if you have some kind of idea in mind, so you can always use a temporary title until something better comes along.

The reason why the title is so important is that it helps you to fix an idea of what you want in your mind. Your course title may also contain a reference to the type of student you are trying to attract. 'Gentle Exercise for the Over 60s' is a good, informative title that will help you focus on content and potential students. I discuss titles in greater detail in the next chapter.

Who are your students?

Your course planning should be done with your potential students in mind. You need to make some pre-emptive guesses as to who will turn up. Once you have a list of the types of student you think might come, then you can begin to sort out in greater detail what you might do in the classroom.

You will need to build into your course plan a certain amount of flexibility, although for certificated courses, it may not be possible to be as adaptable as you would like to be; for courses such as 'Upholstery', you need to be prepared for almost any eventuality. The level of your course may depend on the students you get in your class. If your upholstery class attracts students with plenty of experience, then there is little point at aiming the course at the beginner.

Whilst labelling your class 'for the over 60s' refers to a particular age group, it would be a foolish teacher who assumed that all over 60s were the same. In the case of this particular class, you are going to get a wide variety of ages and fitness levels, as well as different learning styles and expectations.

When planning think of your course as a framework for negotiation with the students. Unless you have to do certain activities for some kind of external body, such as an accrediting body or a professional organisation, what you have planned is not set in stone.

Length and timing of your course

We can't always make decisions about the length and timing of our courses. If we have 30 meetings of two hours on a Monday evening in which to teach GCSE Maths, then that's what we've got. Sometimes, you may be asked to teach a subject in half-a-day that you think needs four years full-time study. On the other hand, you might be able to decide how long your course is. This is always a tricky one. If you have been allowed a free reign on this, it is best to work out the other elements of your course plan and then decide how long you will need in order to accomplish it.

In general, when you teach adults, you will either have a series of short weekly meetings or a day or two of intense work. The course that lasts two hours each week over a period of twenty to thirty weeks is typical of what you might find at your local Adult Education Centre, Community Centre or Further Education College. These have the advantage that you can get to know your students over time, can prepare your sessions based on the previous session you taught and can adapt readily to your students' needs and demands. There is plenty of room to negotiate course content with students.

Increasingly popular, both in work settings and in general adult education are short, sharp, courses. These often last just one or two days – in mainstream adult education, they sometimes take place in adult residential colleges and, for summer schools and the like, can last a week. They have the advantage that you can teach intensively. There is, on the other hand, less room for negotiation. In fact, arrive to teach a Saturday class that lasts five hours and start negotiating course content and your students will probably think you are simply badly organised and don't know what you are doing.

Short courses work very well for subjects that can be broken into neat, discrete topics, or as an introduction. They also give students an opportunity to try out subjects and activities without making a huge commitment.

Aim

What do you expect your students to be able to do in general terms? A driving instructor might expect a student to learn to drive well enough to pass the driving test. The instructor might say that the aim of the course is to 'pass the driving test'. This is a very specific aim, with an easily measurable outcome. The student takes the driving test and either passes or fails.

An aim does not have to be as specific as that. It could be along the lines of:

- to introduce students to computing
- to help students to acquire basic curtain-making techniques and skills
- to improve the students' knowledge of Tudor history
- to introduce students to the works of Bach
- to enable students to describe major psychological theories of education.

Learning outcomes

'Learning outcomes' is a diabolical term that, frankly, makes education sound entirely mechanistic. However, don't be put off by this mangling of the English language, live with the horrendous terminology and embrace the fact that learning outcomes are an essential part of planning a course (and of planning each teaching session).

Learning outcomes are much more specific than aims. If the aim is the overall goal, the learning outcomes are the separate little steps that a student will need to make in order to reach that goal. If you make your learning outcomes as clear as possible, you will find that this will help you in several ways.

Knowing precisely what you want your students to be able to do means that you can plan precisely how to teach them. Good, clear outcomes also mean that you can teach in a logical and systematic way. It also enables you to construct ways in which you can assess your students' progress, which in turn means that they can also monitor their progress and feel that they are learning new things.

Learning outcomes are often written along the following lines:

- The student will be able to play a C-chord.
- The student will be able to name six kinds of perennial plant.
- The student will be able to minute a club meeting.
- The student will be able to wire a plug.
- The student will be able to differentiate between aims and learning outcomes.
- The student will be able to identify verbs in the present continuous tense.
- The student will understand why observing safety regulations in the furnace area is important.
- The student will be able to repair a puncture to a bicycle tyre.

As the vaguest of vague rules of thumb, you should aim for somewhere between one and three learning outcomes per hour of class contact time.

Of course, as we have seen, adult students come to courses with their own agendas. Your course may be designed to teach GCSE Spanish, but in fact, you might attract some students who are simply interested in learning 'conversational Spanish', rather than gaining a formal qualification. Having clear learning outcomes means that you can help them negotiate their way through those elements of the course that are most relevant to them. You might even find that they end up looking for certification anyway, as their motivation changes during the course and they now see it as a goal, rather than an obstacle.

Learning outcomes, for whatever kind of course you are teaching, give you a point from which you can depart. Some students might realise that they need additional skills before they can realistically start your course – perhaps they are more 'intermediate' than 'advanced' – or realise that your course is too basic for their needs.

With some courses, you will be at greater liberty to adapt outcomes to meet specific student needs than on other more proscribed courses. Having a formalised list of outcomes gives you a point of departure and discussion – it also helps to give students an awareness of some of the wider skills that are often needed to be able to learn a subject.

Learning outcomes, crucially, also give you a means by which you can check progress as you go along. This is often vital for higher level courses, where improvement and refinement of existing skills is often harder for students to judge.

Learning outcomes should be written using as little educational jargon as possible. If they are supposed to help students and tutor alike know what they're doing, then don't wrap them round with 'eduspeak'.

Topics

If you are new to course planning, you might like to think about topics first, before getting down to listing learning objectives. I still prefer planning my courses in this way. In fact, I suspect it's the most effective way of doing it. Again, this is where that notebook will come in handy. You can jot down the topics you think need including, but it's often difficult to list them all first time round. Leave your notebook lying around and add to it as and when.

One of my colleagues finds that getting down to the library and looking through the contents pages of relevant books, noting down what they contain, often helps at this stage. Of course, the logical order for topics in a book is not necessarily the same as for a course. The reader has the luxury to be able to skip chapters, re-read and move freely between sections.

When you've got all the topics you think you want to teach in a list, get hold of some paper or index cards and write down one topic on each. You can then shuffle them, spread them out on the table and figure out what you think the best order for them is. Sometimes, the order in which you teach things is fairly unimportant, but most courses, students may have to know something before they can progress to the next stage. If you want to sew on a button, it's pretty handy knowing how to thread the needle first.

Try to think like a student. Forget for a moment that you are a skilled practitioner. What would you find difficult if you were just starting out?

Methods

You have decided on the topics you are going to teach and the learning outcomes you hope your students will achieve. It is now worth giving some thought to the methods you will use.

If you take another look at Chapter 4, you will see that there are plenty of different methods available to you. At this general planning stage, you just need to give some preliminary thought to the ones that you are likely to use. Would lectures be appropriate? How are you going to bring variety to your lessons? What new methods would you like to try out?

Teaching and learning resources

As with your choice of teaching methods, you will need to think about this in greater detail when you get down to planning individual sessions. It is a good idea to think through the resources for your course at this stage as it will help you to focus your mind and make the planning of individual sessions much easier.

- What equipment do you need?
- What equipment would you like to use?
- What equipment is simply too bulky or not available, which will mean that you have to re-think parts of your course?
- Do you know how to use the equipment available to you?
- What handouts, worksheets and other resources do your students need?

For a craft subject you may need to get a hold of various materials or enable your students to find out where to buy them. Remember that they too have local knowledge and may know the cheapest place for certain items. Be fair to your students. There is a horror story of the craft tutor who insisted that students only buy through her. It seems that she was making a more-than-handsome profit on the materials. This is rare. Most tutors buy materials in order to pass on bulk discounts to their students and to give them a range of choice that they couldn't get if they bought on an individual basis.

More general materials could range from photocopied worksheets to overhead projector pens and acetate sheets to chalk or whiteboard markers. Find out what your centre can and cannot provide.

- Do the students need a course book?
- Do the students need any specialist equipment or materials?
- Do you need to prepare handouts and worksheets?
- Are there any other resources, such as CD's, DVD's or study packs available?

Other factors to consider

You also need to bear in mind a number of other factors at the planning stage. Some of these are outside your control; some can only be dealt with by you.

Environment

Find out which room you have been allocated or if you have a choice of rooms. If you are teaching a craft subject, does it have to be a specialist room? If a language, what are the acoustics like, if an art subject is the light good enough? Are the tables adequate for your subject?

Of course, it is not always possible to tell from looking at an empty room if it is going to meet with your requirements. Establish if you can change rooms if the need arises. Sometimes, you just have to lump it. Make the best of a bad job – if the students take a positive attitude from you, they will not worry too much about their surroundings.

Seating arrangements

We saw in Chapter 3 that an important ingredient in any lesson is the layout of the furniture. In some rooms, such as workshops or cookery rooms, the furniture is immovable unless you have a class full of body builders. In most rooms it is possible to re-arrange the furniture. So, if the room you use has serried rows of desks and you want a semi-circle, plan to re-arrange the room. Don't dismiss this element of planning, and be prepared to be a little flexible. A layout that works well with half-a-dozen students might be claustrophobic for twenty.

Eventually, when you have got all these ideas down on paper, then you can move on to the next stage, which is....

Session planning

Session planning is your next logical step. It's also very hard to do if you have never taught before. To begin with, ask yourself some general, basic questions, such as:

- What am I going to teach?
- How am I going to teach it?
- How long do I need to spend on each stage of the lesson?

Don't expect to plan your lessons successfully at the first attempt – it will come with experience. If you are unsure where to start, try this method and see if it suits you. Take a piece of scrap A4 paper and turn it sideways, so that it is in landscape format. Along the top write the following headings:

- Time
- Topic
- Learning outcome
- Tutor activity
- Student activity
- Resources
- Assessment.

Then rule down the page so that you've got a column for each heading.

Time

I am always tempted to put the time in as the last consideration as it can often be the most flexible element of a plan. Typically, each stage of a session should be no longer than about twenty to thirty minutes, but this can vary enormously. Activities should last about half that length.

If you're going to talk to a group, try to do so for no more than ten minutes without some kind of student interaction. On the other hand, students working on arts or crafts projects are often able to concentrate on what they are doing for longer periods of time. That's hardly surprising. Doing something is far more absorbing than being told something.

Topic and learning outcomes

As we have seen, topic and learning outcomes are not the same. Sometimes a topic will last over several sessions and sometimes it might fit into a short slot of a few minutes. It's not enough simply to list your topics; you must say what the students are going to be able to do after this stage of the session that they couldn't do before.

So, your topic might be 'The Origins of the First World War', but your learning outcome for the topic might be 'learners will be able to identify five causes of the First World War'. Learning outcomes help you concentrate on what you are really trying to teach.

Tutor and student activity

It is very easy when planning a session to think in terms of what you, the tutor, are going to do and forget what your students are doing. Looking at the student activity column of your session plan is an excellent way of ensuring that your students enjoy a variety of activities in each session.

If you look down your list and see that all they are doing is listening to you talking, then you need to have a re-think. Similarly, if you find that as you circulate around your practical classes, you are telling all your students the same thing, but on an individual basis, then perhaps you should be thinking in terms of giving a small lecture-demonstration-talk to the whole group.

Don't forget yourself in all this. If you are the tutor, you can't be in full flood all the time. You too need activities where you are not trying to do everything for everybody. Give yourself a little respite by changing what you're doing.

Resources

As with tutor and student activities, using a number of different resources brings variety to your lessons. Don't forget when listing resources that it's even worth jotting down if you're going to use board markers. It may seem like pedantry, but when you first start teaching, it can be nerve-racking and it's amazing how off-putting it can be to forget something simple. Once you're a battle-hardened veteran, it's not much of a worry, but anything that might put you off your stroke is worth avoiding. See Appendix D for a useful list of resources to carry with you.

Assessment

Assessing students is a continuous process. You don't need to give them a three-hour exam after each ten-minute section of the session. You might, however, like to include a little question-and-answer session, or get students to work through a couple of examples before you start out on the next step. As always, match the assessment to the learning outcome. If your students have been working in smaller groups, discussing a text, for instance, they could talk the whole class through what they found before moving on. This way, the informal assessment that is part of our work is done without anyone really noticing.

Evaluation

As soon as you get the chance, you need to give some thought as to how effective each stage of the session has been both in its own terms and in the context of your overall plan. You can then use the results of your evaluation, together with your students' assessment, to plan the next session.

Format of your plan

Some colleges insist that you use a pro-forma plan of their devising. The problem with these plans is that they can be too rigid for what you want to do. See if there's any room for negotiation. If there is, then devise your own. Before you plan a course or a session for real, play around with a sheet of paper and different headings to find a format that suits you. Frankly, I don't think it matters what you end up with, as long as you understand it and it makes reasonable sense to anyone visiting your class for observation or inspection.

As you develop more experience, planning will become increasingly easier. At a later stage, it is easy to fall into the trap of thinking that you don't have to plan. All I can say is that a planned lesson is nearly always better than an unplanned lesson, but we have a tendency to remember those great off-the-cuff lessons we have taught and think we can do it all the time.

To sum up

- Course and session planning are essential.
- Think carefully about what you want your students to learn.
- If possible, negotiate course content and teaching methods with your students.
- Vary your teaching methods to suit your topics and learning outcomes.
- Match your resources and equipment to learning outcomes.
- Assess your students at every stage.
- Evaluate the effectiveness of each stage of the lesson.

8   A professional approach

Nowadays, it is extremely difficult to survive for long in a job unless you take a proficient approach or are lucky enough to be elected to parliament in a safe seat. Freelance trainers are entirely dependent on their performance to keep the customers coming back for more, as are adult education tutors who must retain students if they are to be allowed to continue. It's a tough world out there.

Whatever the rights and wrongs of this, it makes it all the more important that you should take a professional attitude to your work. It all starts in the classroom or training room.

How not to do it

If you want to make your students totally unhappy and get rid of them, you could try the following methods.

Poor planning

> 'Has anyone seen my cigarettes? Only I'd jotted down a few things down on the packet that I thought we might do tonight. Never mind. I'll try to remember, and if I can't I'll come up with something else instead.'

Students can tell when you haven't planned or prepared properly. I think they find it insulting if you're not well-prepared. If the tutor can't be bothered to sort themselves out, why should they? If you work for your students, they are much more likely to work for you. Students of all ages appreciate the effort you put in and whilst school children may not always show it, adults often do. Make it your personal goal to have one of your students turn round to you and say 'You must put in a huge amount of work at home'. It will give you a nice warm glow.

Preparation is so important, that you might find it useful to create a little space for yourself in which to work at home. Many of us now have computers, the internet and so forth. If you've got an office – great. If not, either commandeer the dining-table or see if you can have access to a computer at your place of work. Making materials on the computer means that we can much more easily prepare professional quality work that can be updated as and when needed.

Above all, always make sure that you are well-organised before you set foot in the classroom and know what you are going to teach. Always have a back-up plan. If you're new to teaching, have a back-up plan for your back-up plan.

Lack of enthusiasm

> 'The subject I am about to teach you is so boring that I am bored and you will
> be too. Have I mentioned how boring it is? 'Cos it's very boring.'

Frankly, what on earth are you doing in a classroom if you're not enthusiastic?
I know we all have our off-days and that sometimes you're going to be teaching
through a heavy cold and struggling to make sense. We can't be wonderful all the
time, but in the main, you should demonstrate that you want to be in that room.
Why should your students want to be there if you quite obviously don't? You
really need to show that you love your subject and enjoy teaching it.

Lack of subject knowledge

> 'As you are studying British history, you will all know that the Battle of
> Hastings occurred in...er...er....hang on, I've got a note of it somewhere.'

You must have a decent grasp on the subject you are teaching. You don't necessarily
have to have a formal qualification, but you should know what you are talking about.
   Of course, there are going to be gaps in your knowledge. It's best to admit you
don't know and promise to find out than it is to bluff and bluster your way
through. We're all allowed to forget, have mental blocks, blanks and lapses. If
something slips your mind, or you're asked a technical question, be honest –
someone else in the group might be able to answer on your behalf. If not, make a
note of it in your teaching file and come back to the student with an answer the
next time.

Poor group management skills

> 'If the rest of you shut up we can listen to Maria now, as she always seems to
> have the best ideas and I fancy her as well.'

If you obviously have favourites, fail to treat students even-handedly or don't
cope with difficult students or situations adequately, then you will soon be
perceived as incompetent.
   Managing your group is a difficult process and requires skilled handling of the
individuals in it. Try to be as relaxed and confident about this as you can. I know
that's easier said than done, but you can always fake confidence until real confidence comes along. Feeling well-organised and that you've prepared plenty of
good activities and materials will boost your confidence.

Not assessing students' work properly

> 'Did anybody give me anything to look at last week? Only I've been so tied
> up with various bits and pieces.'

If you teach the kind of subject that lends itself to assignments or homework, then you have a duty to your students to 'mark' their work. You should at least read anything they've written and make comments. If you're teaching a class where they can only demonstrate their skills in class, e.g. rock-climbing or cycling proficiency, then you must make sure that you give your students feedback in class. You must be encouraging when you are assessing your students' work. It isn't going to help them if you are constantly moaning, harping and carping.

Avoid these obvious pitfalls and your life as a tutor, trainer or teacher will be a whole lot easier. You will develop a good reputation for your teaching and thus encourage learners to come to your classes.

Beyond the classroom

Every job of work carries with it a burden of responsibility. Whilst doing a spot of part-time adult education teaching may not be as weighty as running a multi-national company or looking after a ward full of sick people, it does involve certain tasks.

Of course, there is the responsibility of helping people to learn, but your job is not simply confined to the classroom, workshop and lecture theatre or training room. Your other duties will probably include:

- marketing your course
- submitting formal course and session plans
- attending relevant meetings
- professional development, e.g. attending training courses
- administrative duties.

Successful tutors, unless they are such wonderfully brilliant teachers that students and administration will forgive them their organisational sloppiness, also ensure that they do the peripheral tasks to the best of their abilities. So, let's look at how these peripheral tasks help to make you a more all-round teacher.

Marketing your course

Whether you are teaching in a factory or at your local community centre, you will have to advertise your course in some way. Larger public and private organisations often have specific forms for completion in which they ask for information about your course. This is certainly a good step, but often what the organisation wants to hear and what the students want to hear are not written in the same language.

Education and training have become full of jargon and awkward, jarring, clumsy phrases. Students want plain English.

Imagine you're going to be teaching a course on study skills as part of a programme to help adults return to learning. You might describe a learning outcome thus:

Students will be encouraged to develop autonomy as researchers.

That's fine for an internal document or to keep the funding fairly happy, but what does it actually mean to the people coming on your course? Do we know what a researcher is? What does autonomy mean? Are we baffling them with bull?

You will attract learners on the basis of what they read in a brochure, a hand-out or the local paper or in an internal memo. They want to read something written in language they understand. When telling potential students about the course, you might want to rewrite your learning outcome as:

> You will learn how to use libraries and the internet to find out the information you need to study on your own.

When writing titles, blurbs or advertising messages for your course, here are a few ideas to bear in mind.

Choose a good title for the course

I think the best titles tell students what they are going to get. You can get a bit too clever sometimes. Call your public speaking course 'Stand and Deliver' by all means, but if the course is merely listed without any explanation, you're going to baffle people. 'Stand and Deliver – Public Speaking for Beginners' is a much better title. 'Computing for the Terrified' tells us that if we think computers are the most frightening invention in the history of mankind, then we'll feel at home on this course. 'Painting for Pleasure' tells us that it is a painting course and that it is for our amusement, whereas 'Art GCSE' shows that we're going to be studying for a qualification.

There's nothing wrong with a simple title, such as 'First Aid at Work', 'Midday Supervisors' Certificate' or 'Russian for Beginners'. These are good, honest and straightforward. If you're teaching something a little more esoteric, then you can be a little more fanciful. 'Wordsworth – The Dove Cottage Years' may not mean much to everyone, but it will appeal to likely students – horses for courses, and all that.

Use 'we' and 'you'

'You will learn...', 'we will study...', 'you can use...', 'we will look at...' all sound a good deal more inviting than 'the course will involve students in...'.

It will make your course sound friendlier if you speak directly to the reader.

Use active verbs instead of the passive

An active sentence (The boy hit the little girl) carries much more weight than a passive one (The little girl was hit by the boy). 'Future field trips will hopefully be possible,' is not as immediate as 'We hope to arrange field trips at a later stage.' Talk directly to your reader, as I have tried to do throughout this book.

Keep it simple

Use shorter words where possible. For example, why not 'tell' your students, rather than 'inform' them?

Keeping things simple doesn't make them moronic. 'You need to wear loose clothing' carries with it a lot of additional information that isn't stated, but is very obviously implied. This isn't a theoretical class, you will be expected to stretch and bend, not watch endless films of people stretching and bending or making diagrams of people stretching and bending or calculating the calorie-loss of someone stretching and bending.

Make it sound enjoyable

These are some of the phrases from adult education brochures that make the classes look as though you might want to join them: 'This is a friendly, supportive class' – you won't feel like a duck out of water and we're all here to help you. 'You'll be amazed at what you'll be able to do in ten weeks' – wow, not only is it fun, but I'm really going to make some progress. 'We will be working in an informal atmosphere' – oh, good, the last thing I want is to be lectured at on a wet Monday in February.

What is your Unique Selling Point?

Salespeople talk about the USP (the unique selling point) – whatever it is that makes their product different from other similar ones on the market. In your case – what can people do at your classes that they can't do elsewhere?

'Yoga is the ideal antidote for stress' – just the thing after a hard day at the office.

'The Tin Whistle is inexpensive and easy to carry' – great! It's hard fitting a grand piano into a bed-sit and a killer for busking, bring on the penny whistle!

'Try before you buy your own' – the materials can be expensive, so don't buy things beforehand, because one of the first things I'm going to teach you is how not to spend a fortune.

Tell them how much experience they need

'Some word-processing skills would be useful' – they're not essential, but it sure would be helpful if you knew your way around a computer keyboard.

'Students must have gained their Stage 1 qualification' – it's not for absolute beginners.

'No painting skills required' – then it's the perfect course for me.

The local press

Many local newspapers carry 'What's on' listings, where you may be able to mention an upcoming course free-of-charge. It's a simple matter to get hold of the relevant regional and local papers and find out the name of the person who deals with the column or section. This will only give you a tiny listing. A more useful way of drumming up custom for your courses is to try a press release.

Local newspapers are often on the look-out for stories, especially if they involve some kind of success story. A press release is simply a short news story that you write yourself and send to the local newspaper. A press release is not hard to do, but it's worth bearing in mind the following:

- Don't make it too long – two or three paragraphs are fine.
- Make sure there's a story – concentrate on a person and their achievements.
- Send photos if you've got them – a picture paints a thousand words. If Ged has carved a standing oak tree into a fully-functioning model of HMS Victory, it will look great in a picture. Digital images are best.

Advertising your course

Giving talks to interest groups is always a good way of bringing yourself to the attention of a wider public. There are plenty of groups who are always on the look-out for speakers. The pay isn't marvellous, but it's a great way of getting your name about. The Women's Institute, for instance, needs a constant flow of interesting lecturers. The poor soul who is landed with the job of finding a speaker has often been through every name in their guide and the injection of a new and interesting topic is a welcome relief.

Groups like light-hearted talks that still have a good solid core of information. If you can take half-decent slide pictures or have other visual material, this helps. Bear in mind that if you can actively involve your audience in some way, they will remember you and put the word round other groups.

Administrative matters

Keeping all those bits of paper sorted is vital. It may not seem like the most obviously rewarding job in the world, but it helps to keep the wheels oiled. Your line manager will appreciate it and it also makes you feel more organised, so in turn gives you confidence that you are doing a good job. Besides, just because you don't thrill to one element of the job doesn't mean it isn't worthwhile doing it well. If you're not the world's best paper-shuffler, just regard it as the cone you have to eat before you get to the ice cream.

Your register

It is very important to keep the register for your class and to keep it accurately. Whilst a register may seem to have only a limited function as a record for administrative purposes, it can also be a useful tool in the process of evaluation (by monitoring student numbers) and thereby ensuring you maintain a good rapport with your class. There is no need to take a formal roll-call, although it might be worth doing so in the early stages in order to help you and the group to remember names. It is vital that your register is accurate. Most organisations insist that your register is marked straight away in case there is a fire, a bomb scare or some other kind of emergency.

The old story circulates of the slap-happy tutor in the habit of marking the register in an entirely random fashion, who marked as present a young man who at the time of the class was committing a burglary elsewhere. The tutor thereby became an unwitting accomplice by supplying a false alibi. OK, so it may be an urban myth, but it's best not to test it out the hard way.

Attendance and dropout

If attendance at your course is compulsory, you may not be troubled by students leaving the course before the end. Similarly, if you are teaching a one-day course, a short course or perhaps a course at one of the adult residential colleges, you are unlikely to suffer from poor attendance. True, people simply may not turn up, or might have to leave early, but you are not going to experience some of the difficulties faced by teachers of weekly classes. Very few weekly adult education courses still boast the same number of students at the end of the course as they did at the beginning. Student attendance is bound to be erratic as part-time students have competing demands on their time. They may have parents' evenings at their child's school, have to work late, might be ill or have to visit someone in hospital. As a tutor, you need to realise that although a student may really enjoy your course, it is not necessarily the most important thing in their world.

As an Adult Education Centre manager, I once employed a man whose class numbers fell on a week-by-week basis. It's happened to most of us, but he called it 'getting rid of the buggers who don't want to learn'. There might have been an element of truth in what he had to say, but I felt he had a responsibility to engage his students and interest them in what he was teaching. Trying to keep your students is a much better strategy than trying to get shot of them.

You can do a great deal to combat dropout by creating the positive attitude and atmosphere that I keep on banging on about in your class and using as wide a variety of teaching methods as possible. Being perceived as a 'good teacher', who gives loads of encouragement, is friendly, helpful, patient and whose lessons are interesting is as good a start as you can get.

There are also some basic, practical ideas that you can put into use. Make it easy for people to let you know if they can't attend. If you think it's appropriate, give students some kind of contact number where they can leave a message for you. Encourage your students to let you know if they're going to miss a class for any reason. They are bound to have other commitments from time-to-time. Attending your course is probably not their first priority, no matter how much they enjoy it.

If you have handouts and anyone is absent, write their name on the handout and let them have it on their return. Not only does this help students who have missed a class or two catch up, but it also helps to give them a sense of value because you have obviously thought about them in their absence.

The level of attendance at your course and the level of dropout are two ways in which you can judge for yourself how successful the course has been. It is also the easiest way by which you can be judged by other people.

Very few teachers are employed on the basis of their performance. However, adult education teachers need to keep their class numbers; even if purely to make sure that they continue to be employed. For some adult tutors, this may not be too important. There are tutors who have full-time jobs, who simply enjoy doing a spot of teaching, or hobbyists who work on their own and see teaching as a way of meeting others. I'm all for the enthusiastic 'amateur'. They are sometimes the very best teachers you can find, because they sincerely love what they are doing.

You can be an 'amateur', but still take a professional approach.

A teaching file

In addition, it is important that you keep a set of lesson notes, which could include comments on what worked well and reminders about topics the students have asked to cover. Allow yourself a couple of minutes at the end of every teaching session to jot down any little points of domestic business or anything that needs carrying over to the next meeting.

It's worth keeping a note of who's told you they can't make the next meeting or any materials you've promised a particular student. If you're anything like me, you probably honestly believe you'll remember, but by the following week have no recollection whatsoever.

I keep separate files for every class I teach as I tend to teach paper-based subjects and therefore have a lot of handouts and worksheets. You might find that a file can take hold all the paperwork for your different classes. Find any means that suits you of keeping your teaching notes together – the medium is relatively unimportant. Keeping notes, however, is not.

Equal opportunities

There is a huge emphasis on equal opportunities in education at the moment. Successive governments and educators are aware that there are many people who, for a variety of reasons, tend to be excluded from the educational process. Currently, there is a great deal of debate whether providing equal opportunities means creating separate provision for those who are often excluded, or integration into mainstream activities.

As a tutor, you have a responsibility to ensure that your students are treated equally. For some students this may mean that they have to be provided with additional means to enable them to participate in your course.

Not everyone has had the easiest access to education in the past and it is part of your job, in your own small way, to help redress the balance. Find out your employer's policy on equal opportunities and stick to it.

Courses for teachers of adults

Some companies run in-house training-the-trainer courses. These are often excellent, especially if you are going to be teaching one particular programme of study. Sometimes, these are broken down into smaller training sessions on specific topics, such as 'Giving a Company Presentation' or 'Using Visual Aids' or even 'Demonstrating the ZB1098 Vacuum Suction Pump to Potential Customers'.

If you want to broaden your teaching, it is well worth considering studying for a recognised qualification. The best known qualifications for teachers in further and adult education are those certificated by the City & Guilds. The most common of these are the 7307 and 7407, although the numbers and certificates often change. There are also specialist qualifications for such subjects as teaching Basic Skills, Exercise, Dance, English as a Foreign Language and specialist qualifications concerned with the assessment of National Vocational Qualifications. Your local Further Education College is as good a first port of call to look for this kind of course.

Training as a tutor is an excellent way to hone your skills. We can all manage to improve our teaching and improving our status as tutors and trainers. You will also find that the hidden curriculum of your teacher training course is as useful as the course itself. You will meet all sorts of people from all walks of life, who have an enormous range of experience before beginning to teach adults. Contacts of this sort are absolutely invaluable and you will learn at least as much from one another as you will from the course itself.

Professional development also means that you have to stay abreast of your subject. You can do a lot of this by subscribing to the relevant magazines and journals and trying new things out for yourself. It's no good clinging to the twenty-year old textbook for ever; in a fast-changing world, we're out-of-date before we've torn yesterday's leaf from the calendar.

Amateurs and professionals

An amateur does things for the sheer love of them, with no thought of material reward; a professional works for money, knowing that the labourer must be worthy of the hire. Try to cultivate the amateur's enthusiasm and the professional's rigour; you'll find it is a winning combination for teaching adults.

Remember:

- Be punctual both at the beginning and at the end of every session.
- Make sure you've checked the equipment.
- Make sure you've got all your teaching/learning resources with you.
- Arrange the room appropriately, or get your students to do it for you.
- Plan the session thoroughly.
- Tell learners what they're going to do (state the learning outcomes).
- Be flexible and adaptable if things don't go according to plan.

- Be positive about your subject.
- Be positive towards your students.
- Be enthusiastic.
- Be patient and tolerant of mistakes.
- Keep the lesson flowing – if you've got to leave the room, ensure that students know what they're doing.
- Assess students' progress throughout the session.
- 'Mark' any work they do promptly and thoroughly.
- Evaluate the session at the end.
- Keep up your own learning.
- Market your course with flair.
- Deal efficiently with all the boring bits of administration and record-keeping.
- Enjoy yourself if you want your students to enjoy themselves too.

The enthusiasm and professionalism you bring to your work will make all the difference to your students.

9 The first session and some traps to avoid

It's September, the evenings are getting shorter and you fancy learning something new. You did some art at school and enjoyed it, but you'd really like to learn how to draw so that you can make sketches when you go on holiday. A local Adult Education Centre has an art class. The online description in the brochure reads 'A weekly class for students of all levels. Drawing, water-colours, oils, pastels – any medium'. Obviously, it's quite a general class, but it's the only one you can make as you're working when the specialist drawing class takes place. Besides, you like the idea that if you get on well with drawing, you might try out some painting as well.

You have never been able to master perspective, and you don't know what kind of pencils you should buy. In fact, should you buy pencils, or would you be better off with charcoal? Art materials can be pricey. Can you get away with the cheap ones from the discount stationers, or do you need to go to a specialist art shop?

Along you trot to your first class with these questions bubbling in your head. You set off in good time and are the first to arrive. You have brought the minimum of materials. As you slip your single pencil and A6 sketch pad from your jacket pocket, you find that the next person to arrive, obviously at home in the class, is building a small Hadrian's Wall of equipment around herself. She's got a desk-top easel, a full-scale tripod easel, seven trays of oil paints, with realistic blotches in rainbow hues all over them, two boxes of pens and pencils and a folding crate full of old tea-towels, bottles of turpentine, paper towel (with dispenser) and several copies of a magazine called *Extremely Advanced Painting for the Extremely Gifted*. She's also got the eighteen full-scale oil canvases she's painted over the summer holiday – and what's more they've got price tags on them! She knows what she's doing. She slips on a man's shirt. It is paint-spattered and you can also make out the charcoal and paint under her nails. She takes out a quiver full of brushes ranging in size from a single genuine badger hair to external housepainter.

Already, you're beginning to worry. Everyone else greets one another by name. They've all got as much confidence as they have equipment. They chatter away; so do your teeth. You open out your sketch book to make it look bigger and grope in another pocket to see if you've got a biro to add to the meagre collection in front of you.

'I'm going to be working in gouache this term', says one old hand.
'Impasto is so wonderful for expressionism', comes a voice from the corner.
'Did you see the Fauvism exhibition?'
'I hope this new tutor's up to it. Did anyone get her name?'
'Mary something. I'd never heard of her.'

You have that identical uncomfortable sensation as you had on your first day at infants' school. As you look around the class for the forty-third time, you are painfully aware that:

- Everyone else is confident. You're not.
- Everyone else has tons of equipment. You haven't.
- Everyone else is bandying about art terms you've never even heard of.
- Everyone in the class seems to want to do something different. All you want to do is some sketching.

Then in comes another person, laden with yet more kit. You only know she's the tutor because she's got a pink register clamped between her teeth. It's all about to kick off and you need the loo.

Now, swap roles. Instead of being the student, you are the tutor, taking over a well-established class at the eleventh hour. Suddenly you are going to be faced with a sea of unfamiliar faces, each one belonging to a different student with different needs and demands. Some of them may have been coming for years; others are brand new. Some seem to know more than you do; others haven't even brought a pencil.

It's crunch time!

You've read most of this book (even though you skipped the boring bits). You may have taught before. You might have been on a short teacher training course, such as those accredited by the City & Guilds. You know the difference between cognitive, affective and psychomotor skills. You know that you are going to:

- Use the students' own knowledge and experience as your starting point.
- Encourage them to tell you what they already know about the subject.
- Involve your students in the sessions right from the start. They want to know that you care about what they have to say.
- Make sure that they are aware that they can learn a great deal from each other.
- Vary the techniques, methods and exercises that you use in your teaching. It helps to keep your students interested and also means that you do not weary yourself with repeating the same kind of exercise all the time.
- Create a positive atmosphere. Oh, no, here I go again – positive atmosphere. If you create the kind of classroom where people feel valued, where they are encouraged to participate and can feel that what they are doing is fun and purposeful, you are well over half-way to running great courses.

That's the theory – it's a piece of cake on paper, now you need to put it into practice. You are facing a brand new class. The questions and worries niggle at your mind. How am I going to cope? Will they like me? Will the first class go well? What if I get someone awkward? What happens if I don't know the answer? What if there's a fire drill?

Back to basics

Before you start mithering about any of this, it is important to get all those boring essentials right. You need to mull over some of the dull, practical elements of the session. Again, think of your students as customers. Put yourself in their place. If they see a well-organised tutor, then they will already have a positive image of you.

If you can, go and have a look at the room in which you will be teaching. Find out if you can rearrange the room, as this is not always possible if you are using a specialist room, such as a computer suite or a workshop. If you can move tables and chairs, what kind of seating arrangement are you going to use? Will you have to put the room back into its original layout after you've finished? How comfortable is the room? Often, we find ourselves teaching in spaces that are less than ideal. What can we do to ensure that our students are as reasonably comfortable as they can be?

Are there blinds, curtains, heaters or even air-conditioning systems over which you can have some kind of control? There's nothing worse than a chilly room, or projecting slides into direct sunlight.

What are your responsibilities?

Do you need to collect the register or list of participants? In adult and community education, a lot of managers like their tutors to call in at the office for their class registers as it gives them a chance to see their tutors, if only briefly, once a week or so.

You also need to make sure you know the kinds of things that will give your students confidence in you, such as where the toilets, coffee bar and smoking area are situated and what to do in the event of a fire.

Your students

You need to identify any students with specific additional physical or educational needs beforehand if at all possible. Try to establish the ways in which you can help these students. If you are teaching a part-time weekly course, you also need to work out just how responsible you should be. I heard a story concerning an inexperienced young tutor who was taking an exercise class. One of the students in the class had severe epilepsy. The tutor was expected to administer a rectal muscle relaxant should this occur. It's one thing trying to include as many people as possible in the education process; it's another being expected to be a fully-trained nurse or social worker at the drop of a hat.

It might therefore be worth your while writing yourself a checklist of all the things you need to do in the first session.

Time

You should always arrive at least ten minutes early for each session. For your first lesson it is best if you arrive even earlier so that you can prepare the room, sort out your lesson notes, etc. Some students may also be early, having been unsure how long it would take them to get there.

Always start on time. If you are teaching in a large centre, remember that your students may have a certain amount of difficulty finding a space to park, finding the room or might simply have difficulty in reaching the course on time for very valid reasons. It's not a bad idea, if you're allowed to put a few signs indicating the way to your room and a sign stating your name and course on the door. Yes, I know that you'd hope this would be done for you, but for the extra two minutes it takes; it helps create a good first impression.

Equipment

If you have asked for a certain piece of apparatus, make sure you have it; if it is not there find the duty member of staff and remind them about it. However, don't get shirty. Much adult education is run on such a tiny budget that often one person has far more things to cope with – especially in the first few weeks – than is humanly possible. Be tactful and, as you should have an alternative lesson up your sleeve anyway, what's the big fuss? You need the caretaker/site-manager/janitor and the administration to be on your side; you won't endear yourself to them if you start belly-aching from day one.

Actually doing some teaching

The first session is likely to be very different from other lessons you will teach. The group I outlined at the beginning of this chapter is an established one, in which some people may have been coming for as long as ten years or more, although there are obviously a couple of new members. Alternatively, you may be faced with a group of students who are as new to each other as they are to you. It's a nerve-racking experience for you and them. You are going to have a huge number of demands placed on you as a tutor anyway, without the added difficulties of the first session.

Starting the session

Nothing about creating a welcome is remotely difficult. Greet each member of the group as they arrive. It is very important that you create a warm, friendly atmosphere. Everybody learns best if they feel comfortable and relaxed and it will make it much easier for you to develop a good rapport with the class. If someone comes in huffily moaning 'I've been all over the building. You'd think they'd be better organised than this, it's a disgrace,' then you need to defuse the tension immediately. The student's reaction is as likely to arise from nervousness – not finding the room simply adding to their anxiety.

It may seem obvious, but people need to be introduced to one another. You can do this in whatever way you like. You might ask students to introduce themselves and say where they live. You might also ask them to say a little about themselves and why they have come.

Introduce yourself and say a little about yourself. This does not mean that the students need to know your life story or the state of your bank balance, but it does help them to get to know you and feel that you can be approached on an individual basis. It is worth letting students know how and why you are qualified in your subject and a little about what interests you. There's nothing wrong with admitting that you are new to teaching, but it's not compulsory.

Name badges, which can simply be sticky labels, are useful. Circulate a decent-sized felt-tip pen, and then students will be forced to write in larger handwriting. Don't forget to wear one yourself – it helps to make you all equal and students won't be embarrassed if they forget your name.

One trick I picked up off my old partner-in-crime Katharine is to make a rough plan of the seating arrangements and not only jot down the student's name, but add a little bit of description to help remind you who they are. I then try to look at the sheet a few times before the next session, so that I know names at the next meeting. Students appreciate that you have taken the trouble to learn their names and it always impresses them no end.

Students' expectations

We know that students have different expectations of a class and a teacher, so we need to deal with these early on. It's worth warning students that the first session might be a little different from the others because they all need to get to know each other.

One way of ensuring that you can meet students' needs and demands and which also helps to break the ice is by getting them to discuss their reasons for coming to your class. You can, of course do this by asking the class as a whole to state why they have come in front of everyone. You can also give them a little questionnaire to fill out during the coffee break. If, however, you've also got a ton of paperwork that your college wants the students to complete, then sticking yet another form in front of them is asking a bit too much.

At the first session, while you have to spend time getting to know each other a little, finding out the different reasons why people are attending the course and discussing the course content, it is also vital that the students actually learn something. Make sure that the task or activity you set is not so hard as to be off-putting, but at the same time not so simple as to insult everyone's intelligence.

One approach is to pair up students and to get them to make a short list of the reasons why they have come to your class. Give them a few minutes for this, as they will also be getting to know other people in the group. When they've done this in pairs, get the pairs to move into groups of four and to do the same thing again. Depending on the size of your group, you can also do this with eights and sixteens (if it isn't getting tedious). Students will begin to get to know each other, break the ice and this exercise can often lead to some important discussions about the way you will organise your class.

Domestic business

You will have to spend some time in the first session running through some of the domestic business which the students will need to know. This will include fire procedures, health and safety regulations (especially if you are teaching a craft subject), where to go for coffee, where any students who have not yet paid need to go to do so, etc.

Materials

If you have textbooks or other larger materials to give out, now is the time. Most adult students have to pay for their own larger materials, although this is unlikely to be the case in the commercial sector. Sometimes, they may not realise just how costly some things are. If materials are likely to be costly, you should warn students before they enrol. The price of a textbook, equipment and so forth should be kept as low as possible, especially for beginners.

It's also worth giving them little tips if you know where they can obtain things second-hand or if there are cheap substitutes for expensive materials. If you have told students that you will advise them about materials at the first session, make sure that you have brought the wherewithal to ensure that a class takes place. Occasionally, you might be able to bulk-buy something, or have an arrangement with a local shop whereby on the production of a course receipt students can claim some kind of discount. Students appreciate this kind of little bonus.

At the end

At the end of the first session, allow your students time to ask you informally about anything that has cropped up in the session. If two or three people are asking the same question perhaps it needs to be covered at the next meeting.

Before you leave the room, make sure that it is put back how you found it and return the register to its usual place. Afterwards, at home, run through what you did. What worked well? What didn't go according to plan? Was the seating arrangement right? What did you forget to do? Be honest with yourself, but do not be brutal.

Traps to avoid

We all make mistakes when we're teaching. It's a fact of life. Sometimes we don't teach as well as we could. Below are some of the common traps that you should try to avoid.

Not planning fully what you are going to do

The day may come when you can plan a lesson by scrawling a few words on the back of a cigarette packet whilst stopped at the traffic lights. However, to begin with, you should plan as thoroughly as possible, thinking through every detail. This might seem a bit of a chore at first, but you will find that it can help you to think through your teaching in a thorough and systematic way.

Relying on equipment to do your work for you

You are the teacher. Teaching resources are wonderful, but they are not a substitute for good teaching. If you arrive at your venue to find the television you needed for your class is broken or unavailable and you have only prepared to show a film, then you need some other appropriate activity. Always plan for this kind of situation.

Talking too much

Try not to turn your lesson into a lecture. Make sure the students are able to join in whatever you're doing. If you are expected to give a lecture, then keep to time and allow plenty of opportunity for questions and answers. Even if you don't 'lecture', you may still talk too much. And yes, if any of my students are reading this, I know I'm being a complete hypocrite.

The grand tour

A common pitfall for teachers, especially of subjects such as IT, crafts and art, is to spend all lesson, circulating amongst their students, doing the hard bits for them. The majority of students don't want the tutor to do the hard bits for them; they want to learn for themselves. I once went to a painting class where the tutor did some of my painting for me. It might have looked better, but if I'd wanted one of her paintings, I'd have bought it in a gallery.

Break-neck demonstrations

If you're showing people how to do things, don't try for the world land speed demonstrating record. Break it down into small, logical steps and take it slowly. It's no good saying, 'Right then, bosh, bosh, bosh and there's a pretty nifty Picasso copy, mate'. Explain what you're doing. Using the 'Blue Peter' approach and having pre-prepared items showing different stages of a process is not a bad idea.

Not using students' expertise

It's amazing just how much students can learn from one another. A student who has just grasped how to do something, often makes a great, informal tutor for their classmates. Also, if you're teaching a huge broad-based subject such as English Literature, you will find that some students will have read books that you won't have. That's not a failing – it's a strength that the class has a larger pool of knowledge than you do – although not if it is the text for discussion.

Jarring with jargon

It may seem absolutely obvious to you what a twelve-digit flange bore sprocket-holding hoxter with aluminium sliding bolts is and why they have to be manufactured using electro-plasmatic lasers. Your students may never have heard of it. Why not make a sheet with a little explanations of all the key jargon? Make sure you don't use yet more jargon in your explanations. In fact, writing a jargon buster sheet like this will help you focus your attention on how to explain things.

Have a look at Appendix B to see how I've done it.

Worksheet famine

Always carry a few extra copies of worksheets and handouts for when your students lose them. If a student misses a class, pencil their name on any handouts you've used and hang on to them for the next meeting.

My mate Bill

Oh, great. My mate Bill's in the group, so I'll be able to talk to him. Try not to concentrate on just one person or one sub-group. Others in the class will not appreciate it. That's not to say that you can't make friends within the group, just make sure that the friendship doesn't unbalance the class.

Board scrawl

Writing on a whiteboard or chalkboard is trickier than it looks. If you write anything on a board, go to the back of the room to make sure it's legible. If it isn't, either get in some practice or go to the optician.

Thinking it's easy

Normally, when we teach a subject, we are pretty good at it. We probably found it came easily to us when we learnt it. It's often hard for us to understand just why someone is having difficulty doing something so damn simple. Just think about something you're not very good at. How would you feel if you went to a course to study that subject and felt as though you were being left behind?

Under-planning

I'm a neurotic over-planner. I once travelled 300 miles to deliver a training course. The lady who had organised the course stared in disbelief at the amount of material I had with me. 'You'll never get through all that today!' 'I know,' I said, 'but if I've forgotten anything, it's a long way home'.

Have too much rather than too little. No matter how experienced you are, judging how long you need for an exercise is a difficult task and is often entirely dependent on the number of people in your group. If you're as worried as I am, always have the next session planned as well, or at worst take along some additional exercises that will help reinforce a particular point.

Not keeping to time

You may start punctually, but it's easy to think you're giving value for money by carrying on for twenty minutes beyond the allotted time. Your students may have homes and families to go to. If you're training in the workplace, you may be stopping people from getting on with other, possibly more important, work. Be punctual at both ends of your courses.

Forgetting stuff

Nobody's perfect, and you're bound to forget things from time to time. You will lower your chances of forgetting things if you make yourself a little checklist of the various bits and pieces you need in your tutor's toolkit.

I am sure that you are perfectly capable of doing this yourself, but I've made a list in Appendix D that you might like to use as a starting point.

World's greatest tutor

You are now so brilliantly well-prepared that you know when you walk into that classroom you just can't fail. Examine your teeth for spinach, check your fly or make sure your skirt isn't tucked into your knickers at the back; give the impression that you are confident. Then, look in the mirror and repeat after me, 'I am the world's greatest tutor'.

Postscript

Well, I'll have to leave you there, just as you are deciding how you got on with your first class. I hope when you get into the classroom and start teaching it goes well.

That's it for the main body of the book. The rest of the volume contains exercises and some information in the appendices, all of which I hope are helpful. I trust that you have found this book useful and have enjoyed reading it. Of course, it's meant as a simple guide to the subject. It is no more than a starting-point along the route of your own personal and professional development. As you gain more practical experience of teaching, training or tutoring, you will find the theory becomes more and more relevant. Remember, theory is a way of making generalisations about what takes place in practice. It's a useful way of anticipating situations that you may not have come across.

You could do worse than start with some of the exercises in the next chapter. They are fairly typical of the kinds of exercises used on tutor-training courses. They are typical for a good reason – they will genuinely help you towards being a more effective, more professional teacher. They even match the FENTO standards, which is an added bonus for which no extra charge is made.

Don't forget that teachers also need to keep on learning. You might like to embark on a course of professional study or join an appropriate professional association. Meet with colleagues as often as you can to discuss teaching adults. Few teachers are as isolated as adult education tutors, where there is seldom a staffroom and, at best, a coffee bar. Develop new skills; keep up with your subject. Make sure that you gain a reputation as a good teacher.

Lastly, writing a book does feel a little like giving a lecture. It's a one-way process. Unlike a lecture, I don't even have the benefit of seeing your face as you are reading, so I can't even gauge your reactions. It's nice to get feedback from readers, so if you want to contact me, through the publisher, please do so – I'd be glad to hear from you. And please be nice to me, even if you want to be critical. After all, I'm just another adult student, full of phobias and hang-ups, who's a mixture of his own educational failings, terrified of being the slowest or the worst or not understanding what the teacher tells us.

I hope you enjoy working with adult learners, no matter where you do it – church, school, village hall, training centre, community centre, conference room or the side of Scafell. I can think of few jobs that are more rewarding and fun and which bring with them such long-term friendships.

Good luck!

10 Over to you

You will no doubt have been thinking about some of the ideas in this book as you've gone along. Some of them will have seemed obvious, some will be irrelevant to you, and some you will disagree with. Some will be outdated; others new.

Instead of placing exercises at the end of each chapter, I have grouped them all here at the back of the book. I thought this would make the main body of the book more readable. The kinds of exercises listed here are typical of the sorts of things you will be expected to do if you undertake specialist adult or further education teacher training, such as provided by the City & Guilds and college or university based Certificates in Teaching (FE).

If you're not following this kind of a course, you can pick and mix – do the exercises that seem interesting, ignore the ones that don't seem relevant. It's better at least to think about some of these matters than it is to do nothing at all.

Activity 1 – The student as customer

Nowadays, we try to think of everyone involved in any form of activity in terms of the 'customer'. Although there is a raft of debate about whether train passengers, hospital patients and students genuinely are customers, it's still worth putting yourself in the position of a student to get a 'customer's eye view'.

Think about the last time you went on a course:

- What subject did you learn?
- Why did you go?
- Were you sent by an employer?
- Was it a recreational course?
- What did the tutor do that worked well? Badly?
- How satisfied were you with the course?
- How did you feel at the end? Had you learned anything new or useful or enjoyable?
- Did you, or your employer, or whoever paid for the course get their money's worth? Why (not)?

Activity 2 – A student's experience

Imagine you have decided to learn how to draw and have joined a weekly class of two hours at your local Adult Education Centre. The course is scheduled to last for two terms of 10 weeks.

What problems might you face in terms of:

- attending the class
- feeling as though you are making progress
- getting on with the tutor
- getting on with the other students
- practising your drawing at home
- obtaining equipment and materials.

If you were the tutor, how would you help your students to overcome these difficulties?

Activity 3 – Watch others at work

Visit some classes. Find out from your boss, local Adult Education Centre or wherever, if you can watch a tutor in action. Speak directly to the tutor to make sure that it is OK to visit. Be nonthreatening – teachers are used to working unsupervised and your presence could be a bit intimidating.

Make a list of all the positive things you think the tutor is doing. Which parts of his/her teaching would you (could you) use in your own teaching?

Activity 4 – Barriers to learning

Think about your own subject.

- What difficulties might someone completely new to the subject have?
- If someone has learning difficulties or is physically less able, is this going to give them particular problems in your subject?

Activity 5 – Everyone knows something

Ask someone who knows you well (your partner, a colleague, a close friend) to give you a subject or a topic that they consider you know nothing or very little about. Take a sheet of paper and write down in note form everything you can think of connected with that topic. Allow yourself five minutes for this task.

- How much did you know?
- Were you surprised (or perhaps even disappointed) by how much you knew?
- Did you have enough time for the task?

Activity 6 – Getting to know your students

It's vitally important to know your students as well as you can. If you are already teaching a group, think about your current students:

• Who are the people who come to your class?
• What are their names?
• What is the gender mix? Mostly women? Mostly men? About even?
• How many do you know by name?
• Are there certain students who always work together? Does this matter?
• Is the group dominated by any particular students?
• Is there anyone who does not get involved in class discussions?
• Have they studied this subject before?
• Why have they come?
• What do they expect to gain from the class?
• Are there people with any particular learning difficulties?
• Do you have any other observations about your class?

If you don't teach a group, try to find someone who will allow you to observe their class and do the same exercise with their students, or think back to a class you have taken in the past.

Activity 7 – Unsuccessful learning

Think back to an unsuccessful learning experience you had.

• Why was it unsuccessful?
• What did the teacher do wrong/badly/unsuccessfully?
• How would you do it better?

Activity 8 – Learning skills

In Chapter 2, we saw that learning tends to be grouped into three main skills areas – psychomotor, cognitive and affective. Of course, some skills fall into more than one category.

Below is a list of some things you might well have learned how to do. To which category (or categories) do the following items belong:

• Knowing your mother's phone number off by heart.
• How to persuade people to your point of view.
• The six times table.
• How to sew on a button.
• How to perform a tennis serve.
• How to ride a bicycle.
• How to boil potatoes.

- How to ignore provocative comments.
- How to peel carrots.
- How to mow the lawn.
- How to make a stew from a recipe book.
- How to write a CV.

Activity 9 – Your students, your subject and you

- How do you want your students to see your subject?
- How do you want your students to see you?
- How do you want your students to interact with each other?

Activity 10 – Difficult student – a case study

What do you do with an adult student you can't manage and who is damaging the other students' learning and confidence?

You are teaching an English Literature class. One student always arrives earlier than any of the other students, whilst you are busy sorting out lesson notes, handouts and so forth. To begin with, you just think that he is a little lonely. He mainly chit chats about this and that, asking you if you have read particular books. After a couple of weeks, his little chats take a deeper turn. He has by now admitted to being a widower and is new to the area. You feel sorry for him, but there's only a limited amount you can say. Then his talk becomes nastier. He begins to make snide comments about the standards of the other students' work.

It emerges that he is unhappy with the table lay-out (which seems to suit everyone else). In the actual sessions, he starts challenging other students' points of view in too robust a manner. Other students seem cowed the moment he shapes up to talk. You realise that he is attempting to take over the group and wants to show off just how much he knows about literature, giving the air that not only does he know more than the others, but he knows more than you do. You now feel decidedly out of your depth. He is putting off both you and the students. It feels as though he has no confidence in you and is trying to take over as the tutor.

What course of action do you think you should take in order to control this student, who is obviously having such a detrimental effect on your class?

Don't forget – this exercise, as well as aiming to help you with your thoughts and ideas on teaching adults, is also an example of a case study. Case studies are discussed in Chapter 4. You might like to think about how to use case studies in your work. The above example is based on a true story.

Activity 11 – Integrating new students

It is the start of the second term of your course on dressmaking skills. As well as a group of faithfuls from your previous term, there are three new students, one of whom is a man – the only man in the group.

- What can you do to ensure that your new students are integrated into the group?
- How are you going to cope if any of them are complete beginners?
- Do you think there might be any special problems for the man?

Activity 12 – Room layout

Before you start teaching, visit the room where you are going to hold your class. What will be the best way of arranging the room for your particular subject? Draw a quick sketch of what you intend to use. What are the advantages and disadvantages of the layout you have chosen?

Activity 13 – Teaching methods

In Chapter 4, we discussed a wide variety of teaching methods that are available to you. First of all, try to make a list of as many teaching methods as possible without referring back to the chapter. When you run out of steam, you can cheat and look up the rest.

Next, consider each method. Answer the following questions:

- What are the advantages and disadvantages of each method?
- How could each method be applied to your subject?
- Which would you definitely want to use for your subject?
- Are there any that you think would be totally useless?
- Are there any you might consider using from time to time, just to make a change?

Activity 14 – Questioning techniques

Watch a chat show and decide which are open questions and which are closed (yes/no/fact). Are there any questions that are intended to be open questions, but provoke a closed reply? What could the interviewer have done to improve his/her questioning technique? For example, if you ask someone 'Did you have a nice weekend?', your intention is probably to find out something about what they did, where they went, how they found it, etc. However, it could easily be interpreted as a closed question. What other ways of asking the question are there which would ensure that the question was an open one?

Make a list of the kinds of questions you could use to:

- Check students' existing knowledge of a subject.
- Test knowledge informally at the end of a session.
- Get students to think more widely about one of the topics on your course, using open questions.

Activity 15 – Other people's exercises

Find an existing exercise in a textbook relevant to your subject. Look at it critically. Do you like the exercise? If you do, what is it that you like? If not, what do you think is wrong with it? How relevant is it to your students? Would you use it with them? How could you adapt it to use in your classroom? How would you adapt it for any of your students with special needs?

Activity 16 – A bank of exercises

It's very useful to build up a portfolio of your own teaching materials and ideas. Look at the various teaching and learning methods outlined in Chapter 4 and the resources discussed in Chapter 5. Using the examples and explanations I have given, start making yourself the following set of materials:

- An ice-breaker that you can use with a new group.
- A glossary of terms used in your subject.
- A handout giving information (*not* a glossary—you've just done that).
- A paper-based exercise.
- A student-centred, classroom activity that will help your students practise something you are going to teach.

Activity 17 – Assessment

Write an exercise that aims to assess something you have taught without making it obvious to your students that you are directly assessing them.

Activity 18 – Evaluation

Decide how you are going to evaluate your course. Create an appropriate evaluation sheet for this purpose. What do you want them to evaluate and why?

Activity 19 – Planning a sequence of learning (yes, course planning)

Imagine you are going to be teaching a course in your own subject. The course is scheduled for five weekly meetings of two hours each. Make a plan of what you would teach during the course. The following questions are in no particular order, but may act as little prompts for your thinking.

- How would you arrange the room?
- What teaching methods are you going to use?
- How much could you fit in?
- What would you have to leave out?
- What would you expect your students to learn?
- How will you break this down into units, sessions and lessons?

- What equipment do you need?
- What equipment do your students need?

When you have covered several sheets of paper with your thoughts and ideas, then try to marshal them into a logical sequence of learning.

Activity 20 – Planning an individual session

From the course you have outlined above, plan an individual session. In your plan, make sure that you have included the following elements:

- What is your overall learning aim for the session?
- What are the separate learning objectives that will enable students to achieve this aim?
- What activities are you going to use – it is worth breaking this down into the activities you will be doing as a tutor at each stage and what your students will be doing at the same time.
- What materials, resources and equipment are you going to need to teach this session?
- What materials, resources and equipment are your students going to need?
- Who will supply all the materials, resources and equipment? You? The Centre? The students?
- How are you going to assess what progress your students have made?
- How are you going to evaluate the effectiveness of the teaching session?

Activity 21 – Qualities of a good tutor

What qualities do you think go into being a good tutor? Make two lists – one of the professional qualities (e.g. skills, experience, knowledge), another of the personal qualities (e.g. attitude to students).

Activity 22 – Why should your course even exist?

Imagine that your place of work is about to cut 50 per cent of its courses. You want to keep your course going. Jot down the reasons why you think your course should be allowed to continue. Who does it benefit? In what ways?

Activity 23 – Student dropout

Make a list of possible reasons why people drop out of classes. Against each reason, list a series of possible remedies.

Remember, some things are beyond your control. You can only attempt to put right those things over which you have some influence, but an understanding of the difficulties faced by students attending a course will enable you to develop strategies to counteract them.

Activity 24 – The class swot

If you come from a commercial background, you may well have heard of the technique known as a SWOT analysis. SWOT stands for Strengths, Weaknesses, Opportunities and Threats.

A SWOT analysis is not only a good teaching tool, but you can also apply a variation of it to yourself as a teacher.

S   What are your strengths as a teacher?
W   What skills do you need to improve?
O   What opportunities exist for you in terms of resources, methods, etc.?
T   What would stop you from teaching as effectively as you might?

Activity 25 – Teaching journal

You often hear the term 'reflective practitioner' bandied about, especially on teacher-training courses. A reflective practitioner is someone who thinks about their work and reflects on what they have done afterwards. It's a useful idea.

When you first start teaching or go on a teacher-training course, you may be asked to keep a journal of your teaching. Even if it's not part of a course requirement, it is a valuable exercise and worth doing in as much depth as you can.

In your journal, you should keep a record of your own teaching and learning. You should react to the experiences you have as both a teacher and a learner and record your attitudes to the subject you are teaching, the methods you are using and your students. You can incorporate into it your own evaluations of your lessons. If you like, you can also incorporate a regular SWOT analysis into your journal.

It's very easy to keep such a journal very badly. 'Taught multiplication – bad lesson' doesn't tell you a great deal for future reference. Similarly, only recording your triumphs or dwelling only on the disasters is not going to help you at all.

Mapping Your Work to FENTO standards

If you are trying to match these activities with the current FENTO standards, then check out Appendix F. You will see which topics are covered by the chapters of this book and, by deduction, work out which of these activities address which standards – call it activity 26 if you like!

Appendix A: Useful contacts

Adult Residential Colleges Association

ARCA is an association for residential adult education. They have member colleges throughout the country, which between them run more courses than you could possibly imagine. Great to visit as a learner and a useful source of additional income for adult education tutors.

Secretary, 6 Bath Road, Felixstowe, Suffolk, IP11 7JW
Website: www.aredu.uk.net

Association of Part-Time Tutors (APTT)

This is a voluntary–professional support group and training organisation set up in the North-East of England in 1995. The APTT's main remit is to provide accredited training which supports part-time teachers in the post-compulsory education sector. It also helps combat isolation at work and disseminates information on educational affairs. Organised and run on a voluntary basis by teachers themselves. Even if you don't live in the North-East, it is a useful model for organising yourselves locally.

The Membership Secretary, Association of Part-Time Tutors, Wallsend Peoples Centre, Memorial Hall, Frank Street, Wallsend, NE28 6RN
Website: www.aptt.org.uk

Association of Teachers and Lecturers

A professional association for teachers in schools, colleges and universities.

7 Northumberland Street, London WC2N 5RD
Tel: 020 7930 6441
Fax: 020 7930 1359
Website: www.atl.org.uk

Basic Skills Agency

Supported and funded by the Government, the BSA works with a variety of organisations to help people strengthen their basic skills. They also produce a magazine and have some useful resources on their website.

Commonwealth House, 1–19 New Oxford Street, London WC1A 1NU
Tel: 020 7405 4017
Fax: 020 7440 6626
Website: www.basic-skills.co.uk

British Dyslexia Association

Their website is chock-full of information leaflets. If you don't have access to the internet, write for more details, enclosing a stamped addressed envelope.

98 London Road, Reading RG1 5AU
Tel: 0118 966 2677
Fax: 0118 935 1927
Website: www.bdadyslexia.org.uk

Campaign for Learning

A charity that works to include as many people as possible in the learning process.

> 'Our vision…an inclusive society, in which learning is valued, understood, wanted and widely available to everyone. A world in which everyone is seen as having the potential to learn.'

Now that's music to the ears of any adult educator. They also have Regional Offices in Somerset, Birmingham and Warrington.

19 Buckingham Street, London WC2N 6EF
Tel: 020 7930 1111
Fax: 020 7930 1551
Website: www.campaign-for-learning.org.uk

Community Education Development Centre (CEDC)

The CEDC promotes the idea of learning for all – trying to bring about a fairer distribution of learning opportunities. They work with all sorts of groups, such as health organisations, schools, adult education and voluntary organisations. They have offices in London, Cardiff and Northern Ireland.

Unit C1, Grovelands, Longford Road, Coventry CV7 9NE
Tel: 024 7658 8440

Fax: 024 7658 8441
Website: www.continyou.org.uk

Dyslexia Action

Dyslexia Action assesses and teaches people with dyslexia. They also fund research into dyslexia, develop teaching materials and train teachers. Centres around the UK.

Park House, Wick Road, Egham, Surrey, TW20 0HH
Tel: 01784 222300
Fax: 01784 222333
Website: www.dyslexiaaction.org.uk

Educational Centres Association

A voluntary body that aims to promote adult participation in adult education. They also produce a regular newsletter.

Tel: 0870 161 0302
Website: www.e-c-a.ac.uk

FACE (Forum for Access and Continuing Education)

A multi-sector network.

Website: www.f-a-c-e.org.uk

Intute

Free internet resources site.

Website: www.intute.ac.uk

Literacy Trust

'Independent charity dedicated to building a literate nation.'

Swire House, 59 Buckingham Gate, London, SW1E 6AJ
Tel: 020 7828 2435
Fax: 020 7931 9986
Website: www.literarytrust.org.uk

The Learning and Skills Network (See also QIA)

The national resource for the development of policy and practice in post-16 education and training. Now the LSN (Learning and skills Network) which took over from LASDA (Learning and skills Development Agency) which took over from FEDA (The Further Education Development Agency).

Regent Arcade House, 19-25 Argyll Street, London, W1F 7LS
Tel: 020 7297 9000
Fax: 020 7297 9001
Website: www.LSN.org.uk

National Association of Teachers in Further and Higher Education (NATFHE)

NATFHE was the trade union and professional association for people working with those above statutory school age. In June 2006 it joined the AUT to become the UCU (University and College Union). The UCA can be found at the former NATFHE offices.

27 Britannia Street, London, WC1X 9JP
Tel: 020 7837 3636,
Website: wwwuca.org.uk
And also at the former AUT offices at
25-31 Tavistock Place, London, WC1H 9UT
Tel: 020 7670 9700

National Extension College

A useful supplier of all sorts of educational material as well as distance education courses.

Michael Young Centre, Purbeck Road, Cambridge, CB2 2HN
Tel: 01223 400200
Fax: 01223 400399
Website: www.nec.ac.uk

NIACE (National Institute of Adult Continuing Education)

This is the big one. It's the main information and professional service for adult educators. They undertake research, development, publish books, materials and journals and co-ordinate the annual *Adult Learners' Week*.

Renaissance House, 20 Princess Road West, Leicester, LE1 6TP
Tel: 0116 204 4200

Fax: 0116 285 4514
Website: www.niace.org.uk

National Open College Network (NOCN)

NOCN is one of the largest awarding bodies in the UK. They specialise in awards for adults, especially for those who find traditional qualifications inaccessible or inappropriate. If you are looking for a means of accrediting a course, then there are Open College Networks throughout the country.

The Quadrant, 99 Parkway Avenue, Sheffield, S9 4WG
Tel: 0114 227 0500
Fax: 0114 227 0501
Website: www.nocn.org.uk

QIA (Quality Improvement Agency)

'A catalyst for excellence in learning and skills.'

Friars House, Manor House Drive, Coventry, CV1 2TE
Tel: 0870 1620 632
Fax: 0870 1620 633
Website: www.qia.org.uk

Race, Phil

A one-man institution! Loads of stuff here about learning, teaching, assessment. Believer in Plain English. Great stuff on the downloads page.

Website: www.phil-race.com

Ruskin College

An independent college that offers 'second chance' education of a university standard to people who missed out first time around.

Walton Street, Oxford, OX1 2HE
Tel: 01865 554331 (enquiries)
Website: www.ruskin.ac.uk

Support4learning

Fabulous website with great links. A must-see.

Website: www.support4learning.org.uk

Universities Association for Continuing Education

UACE is the higher education sector's association for promoting continuing education. It is possible to join on an individual basis and might be of interest to you if you were teaching at a high level in university-sector continuing education.

c/o Dr. Michael Richardson, Secretary of UACE, University of Cambridge, Board of Continuing Education, Madingley Hall, Madingley, Cambridge, CB3 8AQ
Tel: 01954 280 279
Fax: 01954 280200
Email: smi20@cam.ac.uk

University of the Third Age/The Third Age Trust

Its main purpose is to encourage lifelong learning for those no longer in full-time gainful employment. They organise local U3A groups throughout the country.

National Office, The Third Age Trust, Unit 3 Carpenters Court, 4a Lewes Road, Bromley, Kent, BR1 2RN
Tel: 020 8466 6139
Fax: 020 7837 8845
Email: national.office@u3a.org.uk

Women's Institute (National Federation of Women's Institutes)

You may still think they're all 'jam and Jerusalem', but the WI is a formidable learning institution, with its own magazine and residential college. For years, the WI kept crafts going almost single-handedly in this country. It has around 215,000 members. Talks to local WI groups can also be a useful source of extra income for the freelance tutor.

104 New Kings Road, London SW6 4LY
Tel: 020 7371 9300
Fax: 020 7736 3652
Website: www.womens-institute.org.uk

Workers' Educational Association (WEA)

Founded in 1903, the WEA provides all sorts of adult education opportunities, but is especially keen to support 'second chancers'. They provide over 10,000 courses a year to 100,000 students. Importantly, it is controlled by its members. As well as regional offices you can contact them at:

WEA National Office, 3rd Floor, 70 Clifton Street, London, EC2A 4HB
Tel: 020 7426 3450

Fax: 020 7426 3451
Website: www.wea.org.uk

Useful Links

BBC Education
www.bbc.co.uk/education/home

BBC Wales Education
www.bbc.co.uk/wales/education

Guardian Education Unlimited
www.educationunlimited.co.uk

Times Educational Supplement
www.tes.co.uk

Key Skills
www.dfee.gov.uk/key

NVQ website
www.dfee.gov.uk/nvq

Teachernet
www.teachernet.gov.uk

Teacher Training Agency
www.canteach.gov.uk

Appendix B: Jargon buster

I've tried hard not to use jargon to explain jargon, but it's proved almost impossible. Still, here goes…

Access courses

Courses that are specifically designed for adults who have few qualifications. Access courses enable them to enrol on more advanced courses by providing an alternative to formal qualifications.

Accreditation

In the old days, we tested people by means of examinations and gave them a certificate. Nowadays, there are all sorts of different ways of assessing people. Accreditation is the way in which we can issue a certificate that states that the student has reached a certain standard or level or competence.

Accreditation of prior learning (or experience)

As adults, we have learnt a great deal from life or work. The idea behind APL/APEL is that we can receive some kind of credit for it. There are ways in which we can have our previous experience certificated. Often, they are so cumbersome, that we might as well take the formal qualification that we could pass standing on our heads.

Adult education

Sometimes also known as continuing education, adult community learning or adult and community education – there is probably some kind of difference, but I'm not sure it matters. Adult Education is generally part-time, often takes place in community halls, FE Colleges and schools. Modern languages, fitness, computer skills, arts and crafts often make up the bulk of these courses, although enforced accreditation is morphing the adult curriculum.

Affective skills

These are skills that involve developing and changing our attitudes and emotions.

Aims

Aims are the overall goals of your session or scheme of learning. They are usually quite vague, such as 'At the end of this course you will understand something of the history of Roman Britain'.

Andragogy

Where pedagogy is the teaching of children, andragogy is the teaching of adults.

Assessment

Assessment is concerned with making judgements about students' progress and achievements. In Adult Education assessment has traditionally been informal. Formal assessment techniques are more common with certificated or accredited courses. As Adult Education develops more courses that carry certification, so the amount of assessment goes up. Of course, there comes a point when assessment takes over and students spend all their time being assessed and none learning.

Assessment – criterion-referenced

Students are assessed in relation to a set task or body of knowledge. It is this that decides whether they pass or fail, or what grade they achieve.

Assessment – norm-referenced

Instead of ranking students according to how well they have performed per se, norm referencing is a way of comparing how they have performed in relation to one another. So, the end result depends on how strong the competition was in a given exam or accreditation process.

Assessment – summative and formative

Formative assessment is the periodic assessment of your students to see how they are progressing. Summative is the 'big bang' approach to assessment, where you assess students at the end of a block of learning.

Assessor awards

In order to assess certain National Vocational Qualifications, you may be required to hold a qualification in assessment. These used to be referred to as D32, D33 and so forth. The latest versions are called A1, A2 and V1.

Basic skills

The Basic Skills Agency defines basic skills as 'the ability to read, write and speak in English (or Welsh), and to use mathematics at a level necessary to function at work and in society in general'.

Certification

Providing formal proof that a student has reached a required standard or completed a course. In other words, you get a certificate.

Cognitive dissonance

I promised you in the Preface I knew what cognitive dissonance means. Often, we hold certain facts or ideas very close to our hearts. When we learn something new that contradicts or is at odds with our existing knowledge, we are suffering from cognitive dissonance. For instance, those who think that the battle of Waterloo was won by the Duke of Wellington are often quite upset when they find out it was Blücher who was the deciding factor.

Cognitive skills

Skills that are connected with learning information and knowledge.

Competence and competency

Competence, as you would expect, is when you are capable of doing something. What you can do is a competency. For example, 'The candidate is able to use a hammer to drive in a nail' is a statement of competence, or a competency.

Of course, the trouble with assessing learning using competence is that it doesn't tell us how well someone can do something or if they are truly expert at it. This is one of the real snags of competence-based education; it simply doesn't celebrate excellence.

Continuing education

Often used interchangeably with adult education. It's simply the idea that education is not something that stops, but continues throughout one's life. Lifelong learning is essentially the same thing. Universities often call the department that runs their public access courses (what used to be known as extramural departments) 'continuing education'; that is if they haven't closed them down to save money.

Course

A series of learning outcomes linked by a theme, topic or subject.

Course plan

Otherwise known as a sequence of learning. A course plan sets out what you want your students to have achieved by the end of the course. Different tutors give different levels of detail. Overall, it is probably enough for a course plan to have a statement of the aims of the course, coupled with a list of learning outcomes.

You might also throw into the mix some idea of the kinds of activities your students will be doing, so that they know if they're getting a series of lectures on 'Lakeland Walks' or will be expected to climb Helvellyn.

Curriculum

A broad term that involves some idea of what should be taught. Nowadays, the word is most commonly associated with the phrase 'National Curriculum', which is a Stalinist device to ensure that we try to make our children all the same and merely results in a fatuous sub-standard watered-down grammar school curriculum that is inappropriate for the practically-minded child and not taxing for the brightest. In general adult education, the curriculum would include health and fitness, courses leading to qualifications, languages, arts and crafts and so on.

Dyslexia

A condition that makes it extremely difficult to organise letters into words. Dyslexics are also often personally disorganised. Occasionally, you will hear someone describe themselves as dyslexic when they are quite clearly not. I suspect that it's much better to have a medical condition than to admit that you are too idle to do something properly. We are all, no matter how organised and literate, capable of misreading, forgetting etc. – which is typical of dyslexics. How neat to have a name for it. If someone is genuinely dyslexic, they could struggle and will need plenty of support.

Education

The big tough one. Philosophers, academics and greater brains than I have been attempting to define this for years. I reckon that if you know something, feel something or can do something that you couldn't do before, you've been through some kind of educational experience. The actual root of the word is from Latin, meaning something along the lines of 'leading out from'. The idea is that the tutor has to 'lead out' knowledge and skills from the student.

Educational gerontology

The study of how older people learn. Older learners often underestimate their own abilities. It's true that over time our short-term memories become less effective, but it doesn't mean to say that we can't learn. After all, we saw in Chapter 2 that learning isn't just about memorising, but I'll bet you'd forgotten that by now.

Evaluation

In education, this is the term we use when making judgements about ourselves and our teaching as professionals.

Facilitator

Rather than actually teach a group, a facilitator acts as a sort of chairperson, ensuring that the group moves forward. You will find a great deal of facilitation takes place on courses that involve students in looking deeply at their own emotions. Appalling word – great idea.

Feedback

In education, feedback is the information you give a student after some kind of exercise or assessment. This could range from a simple 'well done', through to handing out the results of some highly complex marking scheme.

Formal education

The kind of tightly controlled education that takes place in schools, colleges and universities.

Functional literacy and numeracy

The ability to read and write at a level that enables you to go about daily life in modern society. Of course, as society as a whole becomes more complex and uses more and more of the written word, the level of literacy deemed to be 'functional' is a lot higher. Numeracy is the same thing, only with numbers.

Further education

Essentially, this means any kind of education that takes place after compulsory school leaving age. However, it is normally used in the UK to describe courses that are aimed at students aged 16–19, generally looking for work-related qualifications.

Handout

A sheet of paper giving information or exercises for your students. Death by a million handouts is what you achieve if you inundate your students with a rain-forest's worth of paper.

Hidden curriculum

If you've heard of the term 'hidden agenda', then it will probably help you understand the idea of the hidden curriculum. This is the unspoken aspect of what takes place in the classroom. In adult education, the hidden curriculum might include increasing students' confidence, providing them with a social network or repairing the damage done to them in schools.

Higher education

This tends to be the term that we apply to universities and any kind of education that is above A-Level standard.

Inclusion

The idea that no one should be barred from participating in the educational process. Inclusion involves broadening access to education to welcome all-comers.

Indoctrination

This is what passes for teaching in restrictive societies. Unless students follow what is being taught rigidly and without wavering, they are failures. It is rare to see indoctrination in adult education; you occasionally see it at the kind of 'training' events that are really small-scale sales rallies that use Nuremberg as a model.

Informal education

Learning that happens when you're not in a formal situation. Typical examples would include learning how to wire a plug from the diagram that comes with it, teaching yourself to play the guitar, looking up your family tree or finding out about Guatemala using an encyclopaedia or the internet. Museums and libraries provide huge amounts of informal education through their highly-informed staff.

Intrinsic and instrumental motivation

Intrinsic motivation is when we do something for the pleasure of doing it. Instrumental motivation is when we have a set aim, such as getting a job or improving a particular skill.

Key Skills

According to the DfES website 'Key skills are a range of essential skills that underpin success in education, employment, lifelong learning and personal development. Key skills qualifications (levels 1–4) in communication, application of number and information technology (IT) are available across all post-16 routes in England, Wales and Northern Ireland. Also available at levels 1–4 are the wider key skills units: working with others, improving own learning and performance, problem solving.'

In other words, Key Skills represent, whilst not the whole story, a serviceable inventory of skills important both in employment and life generally, and for which it is possible to set national standards of performance.

So now you know.

Learning objectives

This term has largely been replaced by learning outcomes. They're not quite the same thing, but it's not worth quibbling here.

Learning outcomes

The stepping stone objectives of a course or session. These should tell students what they will be able to do that they couldn't do before.

Learning styles

The following styles are based on the work of Honey and Mumford:

Activist – likes to get in there and do it
Pragmatist – needs to know why he or she is learning something.
Reflector – likes the time to think about what they're learning, to observe others.
Theorist – goes for structured, theoretical, methodical approach to learning

If you read more widely, you will come across other theories, but this will at least get you started.

Lifelong learning

The traditional way of learning was for a 'front-loaded' model – school, apprenticeship, then real work. Any education at a later stage was unusual, haphazard or even impossible. Lifelong learning is the idea that education is something we need to be engaged on throughout our lives.

Memory – short-term and long-term

Short-term – where we store information that we need to accomplish something immediately. Long-term memory is where we store stuff that we might need at some later time in the future. If you like, short-term memory is the little freezer box in the fridge, whilst long-term memory is the deep-freeze out in the garage.

Micro-teaching

Yes, teaching in miniature. This is a teaching and learning technique that you often come across on teacher education courses. A micro-teaching session involves only a handful of students and usually lasts for no more than fifteen minutes and has an aim and a limited number of learning outcomes. Topics such as making scrambled egg on toast, how to string a guitar, sewing on a button and quick methods for relaxation lend themselves well to micro-teaching.

Micro-teaching is usually observed and often filmed. It sounds horrendous, but can be a lot of fun. It is also a very useful way of thinking in depth about how people learn and how to break up a topic into small, manageable steps.

Non-vocational and vocational education

For years there has been a perceived divide between courses that lead to qualifications or are connected with the world of work (vocational), and those that are pursued for 'leisure' purposes (non-vocational). In adult education, this has always been seen as a simplistic divide. Flower arranging may seem like the ultimate leisure activity. What happens if a student joins a leisure course in cookery and then opens a restaurant? Is the course vocational or non-vocational? I think it is the motivation of the student that makes the course vocational or non-vocational. Discuss in not more than 1,500 words...

NVQ

National Vocational Qualifications. Some people refer to them as 'not very quali-fied', but I would hate to pass comment. NVQs are a government-led initiative to show people that vocational, work-based training and qualifications are important.

Programme of learning

The word 'course' implies that you are going to study something in a classroom or training centre. A programme of learning includes 'courses' in this sense, but also includes self-directed study.

Progression route

Yuck, I hate this term. All it means is the path that you can take to move from one course to another. For instance, if you want to do a degree, you might take GCSEs, followed by A-Levels, then the degree. That is a progression route, although an adult might more typically take an access course to gain entry to a university.

Psychomotor skills

These are physical skills, such as learning to play football.

Question and Answer (Q&A)

A teaching technique where the teacher asks a question and students reply, although with lectures, it is often the other way round – the students ask for clarification of certain points or further explanation after the main body of the lecture.

Reflective practitioner

This term gets bandied about on teacher-training courses. What it means is that you should think about how you are doing your job. This might mean jotting down a few comments about how a class went or which exercises were successful (or not). Teachers who think about their teaching are well on their way to being good teachers. In fact, I don't see how you can ever improve if you don't take a critical look at the work you're doing.

Scheme of learning

This is also known as a scheme of work or a course plan. It is a more generalised plan of what you and your students are going to do over a series of sessions.

Session plan

Also called a lesson plan, but we tend to use the word 'session' for adults as it seems a lot more grown up. It's a plan of what you and your students are going to do in any particular meeting. It will include aims and learning outcomes. You should also include details of the various activities you have planned to make sure you meet these aims and outcomes.

Special educational needs

A huge subject for study in its own right. Special educational needs include all those people who have difficulties with learning for whatever reason. This might be due to a physical disability, learning difficulty or because the learner was unable to benefit from childhood education.

Subject

This is a large area of study and learning, such as Art, Spanish, Management Sciences. Sometimes, such as with the case of 'Art', subjects can be seen in general terms, but they can also be more specific, e.g. 'Water-colour painting for beginners'.

Syllabus

This is normally what is issued by an examination board or an accreditation body. It lists the topics and learning outcomes that they intend to assess.

Topic

Topics are subjects within subjects – little discrete blocks, if you like. If the subject is British History, then the topic might be the Roman Invasion of Britain.

Topic-based work can be a very good approach for adult education, although adults may perceive the word itself as smacking of junior school.

Worksheet

A kind of handout that contains exercises or tasks that students normally also complete on the paper itself.

Workshop

Any class where students are engaged in a practical activity. It is not necessarily limited to craft or art subjects, but can also be applied to any session where you look at the nuts and bolts of something. A drama workshop would be about understanding a play or improving acting skills; a writers' workshop would examine students' own writing in detail.

Appendix C: Abbreviations

The trouble with any job is that it breeds abbreviations and acronyms. It always seems so much more professional to speak in letters than it does to use real words. I haven't just limited the list to the education of adults, but included a load more as well. There are examination and assessment bodies, governmental bodies, local authorities, professional associations and the abbreviations of assessment.

Some of the organisations are defunct, or have metamorphosed themselves into yet another set of letters. But their old acronyms linger like the smell of old football socks.

I'm not pretending I've got everything here, but by using this list you should be able to bluff your way into any sector of education.

A-LEVEL	Advanced Level (now AS and A2)
A2	Advanced Level 2 (2nd tier of A-Level)
ABSSU	Adult Basic Skills Strategy Unit
ACE	Adult Continuing Education
AE	Adult Education
AEB	Associated Examining Board
AEC	Adult Education Centre
AHRB	Arts and Humanities Research Board
ALBSU	Adult Literacy and Basic Skills Unit (now Basic Skills Agency)
ALI	Adult Learning Inspectorate
APEL	Accreditation of Prior Experience and Learning
APL	Accreditation of Prior Learning
APTT	Association of Part-Time Tutors
APU	Assessment of Performance Unit
ARCA	Adult Residential Colleges Association
AS LEVEL	Advanced Subsidiary Level (1st tier of A-Level)
ATL	Association of Teachers and Lecturers
BDA	British Dyslexia Association
BECTA	British Educational Communications and Technology Agency
BAOL	British Association of Open Learning
BSA	Basic Skills Agency
BTEC	Business and Technology Education Council
C & G	City and Guilds
CATS	Credit Accumulation and Transfer Scheme
CBI	Confederation of British Industry
CELL	Centre of Excellence in Lifelong Learning
CETL	Centre of Excellence in Teaching and Learning
CILT	Centre for Information on Language Teaching
CLAIT	Computer Literacy and Information Technology

CNAA	Council for National Academic Awards (abolished in 1992-OUVS look after their records)
CPD	Continuing Professional Development
CRAC	Careers Research and Advisory Centre
CRE	Commission for Racial Equality
DENI	Department of Education, Northern Ireland
DfES	Department for Education and Skills
DSS	Department of Social Security (now Department of Work and Pensions)
DTI	Department of Trade and Industry
DWP	Department of Work and Pensions
EAZ	Education Action Zone
EC	European Community
ECA	Educational Centres Association
EDEXCEL	Educational Excellence Foundation
EOC	Equal Opportunities Commission
ESRC	Economic and Social Research Council
ESREA	European Society for Research on the Education of Adults
EU	European Union
FE	Further Education
FEDA	Further Education Development Agency
FENC	Further Education National Consortium
FENTO	Further Education National Training Organisation
FEU	Further Education Unit
FTE	Full-Time Equivalent
GCE	General Certificate of Education
GCSE	General Certificate of Secondary Education
GNVQ	General National Vocational Qualification
GTC	General Teaching Council
GTCS	General Teaching Council for Scotland
GTCW	General Teaching Council for Wales
HE	Higher Education
HEA	Health Education Authority
HEFCE	Higher Education Funding Council for England
HEFCW	Higher Education Funding Council for Wales
HMI	Her Majesty's Inspector(ate)
HNC	Higher National Certificate
HND	Higher National Diploma
IAP	Individual Action Plan
ICT	Information and Communications Technologies
IER	Institute for Employment Research
IES	Institute for Employment Studies
ILT	Institute for Learning and Teaching
IT	Information Technology
ITT	Initial Teacher Training
JANET	Joint Academic Network
JIP	Joint Investment Plan
JSA	Jobseeker's Allowance
KS	Key Stage
LDD	Learning Difficulties and/or Disabilities
LEA	Local Education Authority
LGA	Local Government Association
LLUK	Lifelong Learning UK (Since 2005 has taken over the work of FENTO, PAULO and NTO)
LSC	Learning and Skills Council
LSDA	Learning and Skills Development Agency (now includes QIA and LSN)

LSN	Learning and Skills Network
MLD	Moderate Learning Difficulties
NATFHE	National Association of Teachers in Further and Higher Education
	(now subsumed into UCU, along with Association of University Teachers)
NC	National Curriculum
NCET	National Council for Educational Technology (now BECTA)
NCETW	National Council for Education and Training in Wales
NCVQ	National Council for Vocational Qualifications
NEAB	Northern Examinations and Assessment Board
NEC	National Extension College
NFER	National Foundation for Educational Research
NGfL	National Grid for Learning
NIACE	National Institute for Adult Continuing Education
NLT	National Literacy Trust
NOF	New Opportunities Fund of the National Lottery
NUS	National Union of Students
NUT	National Union of Teachers
NVQ	National Vocational Qualification
NYA	National Youth Agency
OCN	Open College Network
OFSTED	Office for Standards in Education
OU	Open University
OUVS	Open University Validation Service
PLAR	Prior Learning Assessment and Recognition
QAA	Quality Assurance Agency (for Higher Education)
QCA	Qualifications and Curriculum Authority
QIA	Quality Improvement Agency
ROA	Record of Achievement (now Profile)
RSA	Royal Society of Arts
RSAEB	RSA Examinations Board
S/NVQ	Scottish National Vocational Qualification
SAAS	Student Awards Agency for Scotland
SAT	Standard Assessment Task
SCEC	Scottish Community Education Council (now Community Learning Scotland)
SCET	Scottish Council for Educational Technology
SEN	Special Educational Needs (and Disability Division)
SFEU	Scottish Further Education Unit
SHEFC	Scottish Higher Education Funding Council
SQA	Scottish Qualification Authority
SSA	Student Support Agency
SVQ	Scottish Vocational Qualifications
TEFL	Teaching English as a Foreign Language
TESOL	Teaching English to Speakers of Other Languages
TTA	Teacher Training Agency
UCAS	Universities and Colleges Admissions Service
UCEA	Universities and Colleges Employers Association
UCU	University and College Union
WJEC	Welsh Joint Education Council
WOED	Welsh Office Education Department

If you're fed up with all these abbreviations, then why not join LAGUNA – the League against the Gratuitous Use of Nonsensical Acronyms?

Appendix D: Some useful bits and pieces for your teaching box

This is the kind of equipment that will probably form part of your basic teaching kit. If you are a fully-fledged stationery lover, you will find that it is worth becoming an adult teacher just so that you can go shopping for all the equipment.

If you are lucky, a generous employer might furnish you with much of it and you can spend the money saved on a good night out.

For your own writing needs, a pencil case containing:

- ball point pens – in a variety of colours
- pencil, rubber, pencil sharpener
- felt-tip pens – in a variety of colours
- Tippex/Snopake
- fountain pen, blotting paper and ink cartridges (if you're into proper pens)
- ruler, calibrated in inches for the old folk and centimetres for the young'uns.

So that you know what you're doing in the session:

- teaching notebook
- teaching notes
- teaching file or folder, containing course and session plans
- folder containing handouts
- A4 paper both for your own use and in case students have forgotten theirs
- card
- specialist equipment for that particular session (make your own list)
- diary
- textbooks
- calculator
- spare pens, especially if you're teaching an exercise or craft subject when people might not have a pen with them.

In case anything needs sticking to anything else:

* blutack or equivalent
* pritt stick
* sellotape
* stapler, staple remover and staples
* drawing pins (coloured push-pins are best as they are easier to remove)
* needle and thread
* safety pins
* string.

In case anything needs removing from anything else:

* scissors
* sharp knife
* Semtex (actually you don't need this, I'm just checking to make sure you're paying attention)

So you know who your students are:

* name badges or sticky labels
* the register
* your own list of the students' names (it may differ from the register, e.g. students may not be known by given name or have just joined).

For displays, explanations and boardwork:

* chalk (for old-fashioned venues)
* board markers (check they are the correct ones for the whiteboard)
* highlighter pen
* OHP pens – permanent and water-soluble
* OHP acetates
* spare bulb and fuse for the OHP
* flipchart paper
* flipchart marker
* board cleaner – tissues or kitchen towel can often substitute.

For when you sustain an injury or an emergency:

* mobile phone (or phone card or change for the phone)
* Paracetamol
* sticking plasters.

(You may not be allowed to hand them out to the students, but they're pretty handy for your own use.)

Your own specialist equipment

This will vary enormously according to what you are going to teach, but might include such items as craft materials, disks, lap-top computer or dongle with relevant files stored on it. It's not a bad habit to make your own list of what you need for particular subjects and check it off before you go anywhere.

Appendix E: Personal skills

According to FENTO, which has now been replaced by Lifelong Learning UK, the following personal skills are needed by teachers and teaching teams:

- analysis
- evaluation
- monitoring and reviewing
- planning and prioritising
- setting objectives
- managing time
- research and study
- critical self-reflecting
- identifying, interpreting and applying specific knowledge to practice
- problem-solving
- creativity
- decision-making
- handling conflict
- establishing effective working relationships
- communicating effectively with groups and individuals with specific reference to:
    - preparing effective written materials
    - listening and questioning skills
    - explaining ideas clearly
    - providing constructive feedback
    - contributing to group discussions
    - working collaboratively with others
    - networking
    - interviewing
    - negotiating
    - managing themselves
    - managing change
    - presenting and delivering information.

You can see that this is a pretty tall order in itself. Not only that, but you're often expected to do several of these all at the same time.

In addition to juggling all these skills, you're also expected to 'possess and display':

- personal impact and presence
- enthusiasm
- self-confidence
- energy and persistence
- reliability
- intellectual rigour
- integrity
- appreciation of FE values and ethics
- commitment to education and to learners' progress and achievement
- readiness to adapt to changing circumstances and new ideas
- realism
- openness and responsiveness to others
- acceptance of differing learning needs, expectations and styles
- empathy, rapport and respect for learners and colleagues
- assertiveness.

I especially like the reference to an 'acceptance of FE values and ethics', whilst giving us no indication of what they might be. What happens if they are at odds with 'intellectual rigour'? After all, you often see colleges advertising courses in aromatherapy, astrology or reflexology, which have no scientific basis and therefore are the antithesis of intellectual rigour. But, maybe we're not allowed to say that as it shows a lack of 'empathy, rapport and respect for learners and colleagues'.

You can mock this tick-box approach as much as you like, but when I first started out working with adult tutors, we were inventing our own sets of criteria and trying to come up with lists that looked something like this. Often, the people who came fresh to the teaching of adults had all the personal attributes you would want and simply needed to be given some of the tools of the trade and then, off they went, educating and delighting their students for years. Putting together useful checklists was an important element in that. My advice to you if you are starting out is to use these standards as guidelines, but not to become so wrapped up in them that you fail to see the importance of actually doing a decent job.

Appendix F: FENTO standards

This diagram shows which chapters of the book correspond to specific FENTO standards.

FENTO standard	Chapter No.									
	1	2	3	4	5	6	7	8	9	10
A Assessing the learners' needs										
A1 Identify and plan for the needs of potential learners	*					*	*			*
A2 Make an initial assessment of learners' needs	*					*				*
B Planning and preparing teaching and learning programmes for groups and individuals										
B1 Identify the required outcomes of the learning programme						*				*
B2 Identify appropriate teaching and learning techniques				*						*
B3 Enhance access to and participation in learning programmes	*									*
C Developing and using a range of teaching and learning techniques										
C1 Promote and encourage individual learning	*	*	*							*
C2 Facilitate learning in groups		*	*							*
C3 Facilitate learning through experience		*	*							*
D Managing the learning process										
D1 Establish and maintain an effective learning environment	*	*	*							*
D2 Plan and structure learning activities			*	*			*			*
D3 Communicate effectively with learners		*	*	*	*	*		*	*	*
D4 Review the learning process with learners							*			*
D5 Select and develop resources to support learning						*				*
D6 Establish and maintain effective working relationships	*	*							*	*
D7 Contribute to the organization's quality-assurance system						*				*

FENTO standard	Chapter No.									
	1	2	3	4	5	6	7	8	9	10
E Providing learners with support										
E1 Induct learners into the organization									*	*
E2 Provide effective learning support				*		*	*			*
E3 Ensure access to guidance opportunities for learners									*	*
E4 Provide personal support to learners								*		*
F Assessing the outcomes of learning and learners' achievements										
F1 Use appropriate assessment methods to measure learning and achievement				*						*
F2 Make use of assessment information						*				*
G Reflecting upon and evaluating one's own performance and planning future practice										
G1 Evaluate ones own practice						*		*		*
G2 Plan for future practice							*			*
G3 Engage in continuing professional development								*	*	*
H Meeting professional requirements										
H1 Work within a professional value base								*	*	*
H2 Conform to agreed codes of professional practice								*	*	*

Bibliography and further reading

Bibliography

Abrahamson, M. (1996) *Further and higher education partnerships – the future for collaboration*, Buckingham: The society for Research into Higher Education and Open University.

Ainley, P. (1997) *The business of learning: staff and student experiences of further education in the 1990's*, London: Cassell.

Arthur, L. and Hurd, S. (1992) *The Adult Language Learner—A Guide to Good Teaching Practice*, London: Centre for Information on Language Teaching and Research.

Ashcroft, K. (1994) *Managing teaching and learning in further and higher education*, London: Falmer Press.

Ashcroft, K. (1995) *The lecturer's guide to quality and standards in colleges and universities*, London: Falmer.

Baddeley, A. D. (1997) *Human Memory: theory and practice*, London: Psychology Press.

Baldwin, J. (1988) *Active learning – a trainer's guide*, Oxford: Blackwell Education.

Belbin, R. M. (1981) *Management Teams: Why They Succeed or Fail*, London: Heinemann.

Bentley, T. (1998) *Learning Beyond the Classroom*, London: Routledge.

Bloom, B. S. (1965) *Taxonomy of Educational Objectives*, London: Longman.

Brandes, D. and Phillipps, H. (1979) *The Gamester's Handbook*, London: Hutchinson.

Brittan, J. (1993) *An Introduction to Numeracy Teaching*, London: The Basic Skills Agency.

Brookfield, S. D. (1986) *Understanding and Facilitating Adult Learning*, San Francisco: Jossey-Bass.

Brown, S. (1996) *500 tips on assessment*, London: Kogan Page.

Buzan, T. (2000) *Use Your Head*, London: BBC.

Buzan, T. (2000) *The Mind Map Book*, London: BBC.

Challis, M. (1993) *Introducing APEL*, London: Routledge.

City and Guilds of London Institute (2001) *Further and Adult Education Teacher's Certificate Scheme Pamphlet*, London: City & Guilds.

Claxton, G. (1984) *Live and Learn*, London: Harper & Row.

Ecclestone, K. (1992) *Understanding accreditation: ways of recognizing achievement*, London: Further Education Unit.

Edwards, J. (1991) *Evaluation in adult and further education: a practical handbook for teachers and organizers*, Liverpool: Workers' Educational Association.

Edwards, R. (1993) *Adult learners, education and training – a reader*, London: Routledge in association with the Open University.

Egan, G. (2002) *The skilled helper: a problem-management and opportunity-development approach – 7th ed.*, Pacific Grove, CA: London: Brooks/Cole.

Evans, N. (1994) *Experiential learning for all*, London: Cassell.

Field, M. (1993) *APL – developing more flexible colleges*, London: Routledge.

Fletcher, S. (2000) *Competence-based assessment techniques – rev 2nd ed*, London: Kogan Page.

Gagné, R. M. (1975) *The Conditions of Learning*, New York: Holt, Rhinehart & Winston.

Gibbs, G. (1981) *Teaching students to learn: a student centered approach*, Milton Keynes: Open University.

Gittins, R. (compiler) (1998) *An Introduction to Literacy*, London: The Basic Skills Agency.

Halliday, J. (1998) *Values in further education*, Stoke-on-Trent: Trentham.

Hargie, O. (1994) *Social skills in interpersonal communication – 3rd ed.*, London: Routledge.

Harkin, J., Turner, G. and Dawn, T. (2001) *Teaching Young Adults*, London: Routledge Falmer.

Henson, K. (1999) *Educational Psychology for effective learning*, Belmont CA: London: Wadsworth.

Heron, J. (2000) *The Complete Facilitator's Handbook*, London: Kogan Page.

Herzberg, F. (1968) *Work and the Nature of Man*, London: Crosby, Lockwood Staples.

Herzberg, F. (1972) *The Motivation to Work*, Chichester: Wiley.

Hewitt, O. (1994), *Challenging behavior: principles and practices*, London: David Fulton.

Hodgson, A. (1999) *New Labour's educational agenda: issues and policies for education and training at 14+*, London: Kogan Page.

Hodkinson, P. and Issit, M. (1995) *The Challenge of competence: professionalism through vocational education and training*, London: Cassell.

Honey, P. and Mumford, A. (1992) The Manual of Learning Styles, Maidenhead: Peter Honey.

Huddlestone, P. (2002) *Teaching and learning in further education: diversity and change, 2nd ed.*, London: Routledge Falmer.

Hughes, M. (1993) *Flexible learning: evidence examined*, Stafford: Network Educational Press.

Jaques, D. (2000) *Learning in Groups—A Handbook for Improving Group Work* (3rd ed.), London: Kogan Page.

Jarvis, P. (1994) *Adult and Continuing Education* (2nd ed), London: Routledge.

Jarvis, P. (1999) *International Dictionary of Adult and Continuing Education*, London: Kogan Page.

Jarvis, P. (2000) *Learning in Later Life*, London: Kogan Page.

Jarvis, P., Holford, J. and Griffin, C. (1998) *The Theory and Practice of Learning*, London: Kogan Page.

Knapper, C. K. (1991) *Lifelong learning and higher education – 2nd ed*, London: Kogan Page.

Knowles, M. (1978) *The Adult Learner: A Neglected Species*, Houston: Gulf.

Kolb, D. A. (1984) *Experiential Learning: Experience as the Source of Learning and Development*, London: Prentice Hall.

Kyriacou, C. (2001) *Essential Teaching skills 2nd ed.*, Cheltenham: Nelson Thornes.

Levinson, D. (1979 re-issue) *The Seasons of a Man's Life*, New York: Ballantine Books.

Levinson, D. (1997) *The Seasons of a Woman's Life*, New York: Ballantine Books.

Lewis, V. (1995) *53 interesting ways to promote equal opportunities in education – rev. ed*, Bristol: Technical and Educational Services.

Loughran, J. (1999) *Researching teaching: methodologies and practices for understanding pedagogy*, London: Falmer Press.

Maclure, S. (1991) *Missing links – the challenges to further education*, London: Policy Studies Institute.

McGivney, V. (1993) *Women, education and training – barriers to access, informal starting points*, Leicester: NIACE in association with Hillcroft College

Maslow, A. H. (1968) *Towards a Psychology of Being*, New York: Van Nostrand.

Merriam, S.B., and Clark, M.C. (1991) Lifetimes: Patterns of Work, Love, and Learning in Adulthood. San Francisco: Jossey-Bass.

Minton, D. (1991) *Teaching Skills in Further and Adult Education*, Basingstoke: City & Guilds/Macmillan.

Mitchell, P. (1998) *Beyond the universities: the new higher education*, Aldershot: Ashgate.

Moon, J. (2000) *Short Courses and Workshops—Improving the Impact of Learning, Training and Professional Development*, London: Kogan Page.

Morris, D. (1978) *Manwatching*, London: Panther Books.

Nasta, A (1994) *How to design a vocational curriculum: a practical guide for schools and colleges*, London: Kogan Page.

Nyatanga, L. (1998), *Good practice in the accreditation of prior learning*, London: Cassell.

Petty, G. (2004) *Teaching today: a practical guide – 3rd ed*, Cheltenham: Nelson Thornes.

Race, P. (ed) (1999) *2000 Tips for Lecturers*, London: Kogan Page.

Race, P. and Brown, S. (1993) *500 Tips for Tutors*, London: Kogan Page.

Race, P. and Brown, S. (2000) *500 Tips on Group Learning*, London: Kogan Page.

Race, P. and Smith, B. (1995) *500 Tips for Trainers*, London: Kogan Page.

Race, P. (2001) *The Lecturer's Toolkit*, London: Kogan Page.

Raggatt, P. (1996) *The Learning society: challenges and trends*, London: Routledge in association with the Open University.

Reece, I. and Walker, S. (2000) Teaching, Training and Learning, Sunderland: Business Education Publishers Ltd.

Rogers, A. (1996) *Teaching Adults*, Buckingham: Open University Press.

Rogers, C. (1994), *Freedom to learn – 3rd ed*, Upper Saddle River, NJ: Merrill.

Rogers, J. (2001) *Adults Learning* (4th ed), Buckingham: Open University Press.

Rogerson, S. (1996) *Successful group work*, London: Kogan Page (in association with De Montfort University).

Rowntree, D. (1990) *Teaching through self-instruction: how to develop open learning materials – rev. ed*, London: Kogan Page.

Sallis, E. J. (2002) *Total quality management in education – 3rd ed.*, London: Kogan Page.

Schön, D. (1983) *The Reflective Practitioner: How Professionals Think in Action*, New York: Basic Books.

Silverman, D. (2001) *Interpreting qualitative data: methods for analyzing talk, text and interaction – 2nd ed.*, London: SAGE.

Stephens, M. (1990) *Adult education*, London: Cassell.

Sutherland, P. (1998) *Adult learning – a reader*, London: Kogan Press.

Thorpe, M. (1993) *Culture and processes of adult learning – a reader*, London: Routledge in association with the Open University.

Tight, M. (1996) *Key Concepts in Adult Education and Training*, London: Routledge.

Tight, M. (1998) *Adult Learning and Education*, London: Routledge.

Torrance, H. (1998) *Investigating formative assessment: teaching, learning and assessment in the classroom*, Buckingham: Open University Press.

Walford, G. (1998) *Doing research about education*, London: Falmer Press.

Walklin, L. (1990) *Teaching and learning in further and adult education*, Cheltenham: Stanley Thornes.

Wellington, J. (1996) *The work related curriculum: challenging the vocational imperitive*, London: Kogan Page.

Woods, P. (1996) *Contemporary issues in teaching and learning*, London; New York: Routledge in association with the Open University.

Some alternative suggestions for reading and viewing

I suspect that there is as much to be learned by reading books and watching films that deal intelligently with education and human behaviour. Forget the kind of film where our embattled hero takes on a class of thirty psychopaths and turns them into literary geniuses (or genii), they're just tedious; but some books and films that you might like to think about could include such classics as:

Pygmalion by George Bernard Shaw. We all know the basic story of Shaw's *Pygmalion*, because we've seen *My Fair Lady*. The original play is more useful to you as a tutor. Like the Pygmalion of myth, Professor Higgins falls in love with his 'creation'.

Educating Rita by Willie Russell is an updated version of the story, but shows how education can be both liberating and a burden. Whilst Frank, the drunken university lecturer, may have fallen in love with the gobby Rita, he (eventually) helps to sets her mind free, rather than simply moving her into a different social class.

A Clockwork Orange by Anthony Burgess shows how you can destroy the good in someone along with the evil.

Lord of the Flies by William Golding. Without proper forms of organisation, groups can go appallingly wrong. Golding was, I believe, a Preparatory Schoolmaster. He had to leave his class for a few minutes and came back to find a riot going on. The book is essentially about how adults bring order, but shows how badly things can deteriorate. Mind you, you can watch plenty of reality television shows to witness just the same.

On the other hand, *Animal Farm* and *1984* by George Orwell, and *One Flew over the Cuckoo's Nest* by Ken Kesey, show just how organisations can ruin lives if they attempt to control too strongly.

The Education of Hyman Kaplan by Leo Rosten tells the story of Hyman Kaplan, everyone's nightmare student. The book also demonstrates just how difficult English can be as our immigrant hero gets to grips with his new language.

Sophie's World by Jostein Gaardner gives an introduction to philosophical ideas.

Any books by Nicholas Corder are worth buying as the poor man needs as much money as he can if he's ever to live that jet-set life-style.

Other publications that might be of use

The National Institute for Adult and Continuing Education (NIACE) publishes *a range of materials, including The Adult Learning Yearbook and a magazine*

Adults Learning, which produces ten issues per year, covering the education and training of adults—there is a reduced price for part-time lecturers and students.

Hobsons publish the *Directory of Further Education*.

Kogan Page publish an *International Directory of Adult and Continuing Education*.

ARCA (The Adult Residential Colleges Association) produces a book listing residential courses under the title *Time to Learn*.

Index